# The ARIZONA *Celebrity* COOKBOOK

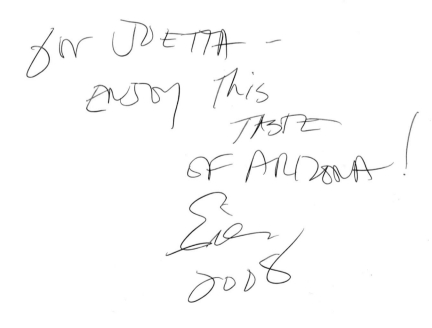

for Joetta —

Enjoy this

Taste

of Arizona!

2008

# The ARIZONA *Celebrity* COOKBOOK

*by* **EILEEN BAILEY**

*photographs by* **DANA LEONARD**

A portion of the proceeds benefits *The Arizona Republic*'s Season for Sharing campaign.

**NORTHLAND PUBLISHING**

SEASON FOR SHARING
THE ARIZONA REPUBLIC

A portion of the proceeds benefits *The Arizona Republic*'s Season for Sharing campaign and will be used to support Arizona agencies that serve the hungry. Season for Sharing is a fund of the Robert R. McCormick Tribune Foundation.

The text type was set in Cochin
The display type was set in Copperplate and Sloop
Composed in the United States of America
Designed by Rudy J. Ramos
Edited by Jody Berman and Stephanie Bucholz
Production supervised by Lisa Brownfield

Printed in Hong Kong by
Wing King Tong Company Limited

FIRST IMPRESSION
ISBN 0-87358-692-1

Library of Congress Catalog Card Number 97-24702
Bailey, Eileen.
The Arizona celebrity cookbook / by Eileen Bailey;
photographs by Dana Leonard. — 1st ed.
p.   cm.
ISBN 0-87358-692-1
1. Cookery, American.  2. Celebrities—Arizona.
I. Title.
TX715.B1483  1997
641.5973—dc21                    97-24702

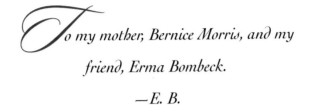

*To my mother, Bernice Morris, and my friend, Erma Bombeck.*

—E. B.

*To Nancy Engebretson, without whose help this book would not have been possible.*

—D. L.

# $\mathcal{C}$ontents

ACKNOWLEDGMENTS, *viii*

INTRODUCTION, *1*

Danielle Ammaccapane, *2*

Bill Andres, *4*

Joe Arpaio, *6*

Eddie Basha, *8*

The Bombeck Family, *10*

Sam Campana, *12*

Glen Campbell, *14*

Michael Carbajal, *16*

Carol Cavazos, *18*

Anne Coe, *20*

Jerry Colangelo, *22*

Ike Cole, *24*

Sheryl Cooper, *26*

Lattie Coor, *28*

Clive Cussler, *30*

Perry Damone, *32*

Kent Dana, *34*

Rita Davenport, *36*

Hugh Downs, *38*

Herb Drinkwater, *40*

Tex Earnhardt, *42*

Al Feinberg, *44*

Bill Frieder, *46*

Joe Garagiola, *48*

Terry Goddard, *50*

Barry Goldwater Jr., *52*

R. C. Gorman, *54*

Zarco Guerrero, *56*

Paul Hamilton, *58*

Bill Heywood, *60*

Tara Hitchcock, *62*

Geordie Hormel, *64*

Jane Dee Hull, *66*

Waylon Jennings, *68*

Bil Keane, *70*

Jon Kyl, *72*

G. Gordon Liddy, *74*

Clara Lovett, *76*

Harvey Mackay, *78*

Merrill Mahaffey, *80*

Robert McCall, *82*

Al McCoy, *84*

Beth McDonald, *86*

Dorothy McGuire
    Williamson, *88*

Pat McMahon, *90*

Ed Mell, *92*

Ann Miller, *94*

Jim Mitchum, *96*

Rose Mofford, *98*

Sam Moore, *100*

Lute Olson, *102*

Pete Pearson, *104*

Valerie Perrine, *106*

Dave Pratt, *108*

Francine Reed, *110*

Skip Rimsza, *112*

Fritz Scholder, *114*

Doc Severinsen, *116*

Robert Shields, *118*

Debbie Sledge, *120*

Sam Steiger, *122*

Ann Symington, *124*

Marshall Trimble, *126*

Jesse Valenzuela, *128*

Tom Weiskopf, *130*

Preston Westmoreland, *132*

Paul Westphal, *134*

Grant Woods, *136*

INDEX, *138*

# Acknowledgments

SO MANY FRIENDS have put their mark on this book. First, I'd like to thank photographers Dana Leonard and Nancy Engebretson for their great work in capturing the essence of the subjects. It's said that the mark of a true pro is making something look easy, and Dana and Nancy made each photo session look like a walk in the park; that is, assuming you're schlepping tons of gear to the park.

Others who helped tremendously were Alison Goldwater Ross, Bob Corritore, Marie Pepicello, Mike Clancy, Susan Heywood, June Westgaard, Kim Campbell, Sheryl Cooper, Sheila Thatcher, Vincent Guerithault, Edith Kunz, Ed Mell, Julie Fie, Ralph Ammaccapane, Elva Coor, Jackie Drinkwater, Rebecca Reeves, Florenz Sledge, Judy Miner, Girley Reed, Patricia Myers, Gina Bridgeman, Jean Ferrari, Paula Meadow, John Driscoll, Mark Tarbell, Laura Fraenza, John Popp, Judy Walker, Dave Walker, Joyce Moore, Carol Bidstrup, Rose Roybal, Virginia Dooley, Leslie Tweeton, Pam Barbey, Jamie Hormel, Barbara Fenzl, Kitty Kelley, Linda Bailey Starr, Harriet Friedland, Dodie Johnes, Del and Jewell Lewis, Jessi Ringeisen from McAlpine Soda Fountain, and Boyd Orth.

I also appreciate the support of my daughters, Kelly Calzaretta, Shelly Mullins, and Laurie Brooks Flores.

David Jenney and Erin Murphy of Northland Publishing were fabulous to work with, as were Rudy Ramos, Karen Anderson, and Linda Kranz.

Northland, established in 1958 by Paul Weaver, is one of Arizona's real treasures.

# *Introduction*

TELL ME WHAT you eat and I will tell you what you are," wrote Brillat Savarin. M. F. K. Fisher said, "Almost every person has something secret he likes to eat."

They're right. Ask someone what they eat and find out who they really are. I've learned there's no quicker way to get to know someone.

People get downright revealing—and funny—when they discuss the way they feel about food.

This book evolved from a column I've written for *The Arizona Republic* over the past few years. "You know everyone," said my then-editor, Jane See White. "Why don't you do a food column on what well-known people eat?"

I did. It caught on, and a book seemed only natural.

The interviews I conducted were a constant source of surprise. And delight. I laughed my way through the project.

I was an unwitting straight man to Glen Campbell. Me: "Is your wife a good cook? Glen: "Well, let me put it this way. A swarm of flies got together and fixed the screen door."

Author Clive Cussler confided that while eating lengthy gourmet meals in European capitols, he dreamed of a simple "peanut-butter-and-mayonnaise sandwich with a big dill pickle."

Sheriff Joe Arpaio told me his all-time peak dining experience is "a baloney sand-wich made by the jail chef." (Isn't *jail chef* an oxymoron? Or is that just Joe?)

I asked G. Gordon Liddy whether he ever had any midnight cravings. He replied, perfectly straight-faced, "All my midnight cravings are for sex."

Discussing fast food, Joe Garagiola said his idea of a balanced meal is "not dropping it when you walk to the car."

I discovered what poor really means. Waylon Jennings' dad "worked sunup to sundown for a dollar a day." When Waylon was a toddler, "we walked down to this man's house and he gave us something to eat. It was the first time I ever saw a refrigerator and linoleum. At home we had a dirt floor."

What foods are most hated? Liver was the overwhelming winner (loser?) in that category. During the 1940s and '50s, many mothers across the country made liver once a week, some of them, like Carol Cavazos's mom, "cooking the heck out of it."

Bill Andres feels like vomiting when he drinks tomato juice. Francine Reed used to hate olives: "But I put them in martinis now," she said, "and they're not bad at all."

Some people are guilty about their food habits. "We're sort of TV people," said Robert McCall, "and we feel a certain guilt about having it on during dinner."

Others bragged about their bad food habits. "I never had a salad until I was probably thirty," said Grant Woods. "I've had maybe two or three apples in my life."

A visit to the White House impressed Barry Goldwater, Jr. "not so much for the food," but the aura of power, "and every time I went to the White House, I stole something—an ashtray or a spoon."

In several cases, the interviews conjured up images of an Arizona gone by. "A real treat was to go to the Carnation store on North Central," said Kent Dana.

Marshall Trimble talked of his hometown, Ashfork. "It had a soda fountain, a picture show, a pool hall, and it even had the Harvey House; what else do you need?" What indeed?

Not everyone cooks, I found. "Let's put it this way," said former governor Rose Mofford, "I have a brand new stove which I had put in twenty years ago. When it's sold, the ad could say, 'a new stove that's never been used by a little old lady from Globe.'"

Some of my friends have said, "Eileen Bailey writing a cookbook? She's no cook. Why, she had Carol Steele's whole family over one time, and sent out for pizza! When she got married, all she could cook was baked Spam. She once served what looked like Elmer's Glue Fondue. Her daughters say the only thing she can make is reservations."

True. But I can write. And I can cajole everybody who's anybody into being in my book, can't I?

Besides, there's a reason God invented take-out.

# Danielle Ammaccapane

Pro golfer Danielle Ammaccapane grew up in Phoenix, and has played golf since she was ten, "seriously" since she was fourteen. She has won several major Ladies' Professional Golf Association events, including the Standard Register Ping, Mitsubishi Pro-Am, Centel Classic, and Hershey Tournament.

Though she is known for golf, her family is known for food. Her father, Ralph, owns Ammaccapane's Restaurant and Sports Bar at Seventh Street and Thunderbird in Phoenix. Her grandfather, also named Ralph, had Raffaele's Arbor at Central and Dunlap for many years; now eighty-two, he lives on Long Island, where he operated a pizzeria until last year.

Ammaccapane lives in Phoenix with her husband, Rod Kesling.

*I don't have to ask what you ate as a child, do I?*

We had meatballs and pastas and sausage. My mom made us eat vegetables, too. Once in awhile she'd make meat loaf or something, but mostly it was Italian food. She's Italian, too, and a real good cook.

*What's the first thing you remember cooking?*

Fresh sauce. My sister and I were told, "If you can make this, you can always eat." It's way better than those horrible jars of sauce. There's no secret to it, no teaspoon of this, tablespoon of that. You just brown a little garlic in a little oil, add a can of tomatoes, some oregano, parsley, and basil, and that's it. You can add whatever else you want.

*Ever have any cooking disasters?*

One time I broiled some cookies instead of baking them. Another time I overcooked the meat loaf. We ate it but it was horrible.

*Do you cook much now?*

I'm starting to. Rod likes to cook, too. We travel so much that the last thing we want to do when we get home is go out.

*What do you like to eat?*

Fish, seafood, Caesar salads. I'm throwing a beef stew into the Crock-Pot right now. I'm not a real health nut, and I don't have to watch my weight but I eat pretty well.

*Do you eat any sinful foods?*

I like some ice cream, chips, and Reese's candy, but I don't go off and attack something really bad. I eat until I'm full. I don't like chocolate or cake. Pumpkin pie I love, but I just eat in moderation.

*Where was your peak dining experience?*

I'll tell you exactly where. It was in Zermatt, Switzerland, on our honeymoon in January 1996. We had this shrimp dish with garlic and rice at this cozy little place with a fireplace. I'll remember that forever. I came back and told my dad, "If you could master this dish, we'd be very rich."

## AMMACCAPANE'S LINGUINE WITH CLAM SAUCE

16 ounces linguine
⅓ cup olive oil
4 garlic cloves, minced
  or mashed
2 (6½-ounce) cans chopped
  clams, undrained
1 teaspoon chopped fresh parsley
  (or ½ teaspoon dried)
Dash of black pepper
Pinch of salt

*Boil the linguine while making the sauce.*

*In a medium-size skillet, sauté the garlic in the oil until golden brown. Throw in the clams, clam juice, parsley, pepper, and salt. Bring to a boil (don't heat longer or clams will get tough). Pour over the cooked linguine.*
*Serves 4.*

# Bill Andres

Radio personality Bill Andres grew up in Ohio and is a 1975 graduate of the University of Dayton. With his on-air partner, John Giese, he was responsible for the success of KDKB's morning show in the late 1970s and later created winning formats for several other Valley radio and television stations.

Andres is an active community volunteer, serving on the boards of the Foundation for Burns and Trauma and the Arizona Children's Burn Camp.

He and his wife, Elizabeth, live in Phoenix with their sons: William, ten, and Eric, six.

**Did you cook when you were a kid?**

Oh, sure. The first thing I made was probably a fried baloney sandwich or a sheet cake. But I have three older sisters so I didn't cook much. When I went to college, I lived with three other guys, and my specialties were chili, lasagna, and burritos. When I became a vegetarian twenty years ago, I had to learn to cook all over again.

**Do you cook now?**

No, I married the world's best cook, so the most I cook now is fried eggs on Saturday morning. Man food.

**Ever have any cooking disasters?**

Hasn't everybody boiled the vegetables dry until the pan is black and smoking?

**What's your favorite fast food?**

The fish tacos at Filiberto's. And Taco Bell's green bean burrito. That's not with green beans, by the way.

**What's the best meal you ever ate?**

A few years ago, we were back East, touring New England, and we bought six or eight of those lobsters they call chickens—each one weighs a pound or more. We called my folks on the way and said, "Start boiling water." It was a real family feast.

**Any foods you hate?**

I'm not sure why, but I want to vomit if I look at or drink tomato juice.

**What's your favorite sinful food?**

Nature's most nearly perfect food: green peanut M&Ms. That's not green peanuts, by the way.

**Where do you like to eat out?**

The Tee Pee, P. F. Chang's, Sam's Cafe, and it's always fun to take the kids to Ed Debevic's.

**What would you choose for your last meal?**

A chile relleno from the Tee Pee, a glass of Golden Amber from Coyote Springs Brewing, a salad niçoise from Sfuzzi, and a five-pound bag of peanut M&Ms. If it's my last meal, I'd want it to kill me!

## BILL'S CAMPFIRE HALIBUT

*This recipe uses one of the world's most abundant food sources: Taco Bell hot sauce.*

*What you do, see, is, on your way to the Rim or wherever you're camping, you pick up a nice halibut steak, and stop by Taco Bell to pick up some packets of their hot, hot sauce.*

*Then you marinate the fish in 2 parts Taco Bell hot, hot sauce (you can substitute Arby's Horsey Sauce), 1 part ketchup, the juice of 1 lemon, and 1 part tequila (any call brand will do, like Loma Viejo, which, as you know, means "old dirt" in Spanish).*

*While you're marinating the fish, you build a fire, and when it's going good, toss a couple of foil-wrapped potatoes on the grill. Half an hour later, put the fish on, taking care not to let the marinade drip on the flame. Cook 4 to 6 minutes per side.*

*To get really fancy, you can also boil a can of peas. This is good with a nice chardonnay. And relish. I go to festivals to pick up little packets of relish. They keep a long time in your mess kit.*

*Serves 1.*

# Joe Arpaio

Maricopa county sheriff Joe Arpaio was raised in Springfield, Missouri, where his father had an Italian grocery. His parents came to the United States from Naples in 1918.

After serving as a police officer in Washington, D.C., and Las Vegas, Nevada, Arpaio joined the Federal Drug Enforcement Administration in 1957. He worked for the DEA in Turkey, Mexico, the Middle East, and throughout the United States for twenty-seven years. He briefly joined his wife, Ava, in her travel agency, Starworld, before running for sheriff in 1992. The Arpaios have two grown children, Rocco and Sherry.

In the five years that Arpaio has been Maricopa County sheriff, he has received international attention for his unorthodox practices: he has formed a *civilian "posse"; inmates must wear pink underwear and are not allowed coffee; and many inmates live in Arpaio's so-called Tent City, which he has decorated with a large "Vacancy" sign.*

---

*How'd you learn to cook?*

I didn't. I burn water.

*What's your favorite sinful food?*

Bread and water.

*Your favorite healthful food?*

Whole wheat bread and water.

*What's your favorite fast food?*

Coffee. I don't eat breakfast, I skip lunch, and since I work fourteen to fifteen hours a day, I usually eat dinner on the road. I seldom get home for a cooked meal. I worked four years in Mexico, so I like Taco Bell.

*Your all-time peak culinary experience?*

Baloney sandwiches made by the jail chef. Other than baloney, I really like linguine and calamari. I'm Italian, you know.

*What foods do you eat?*

Not that I'm heavy but I have to watch my intake. I'm jealous of those who can eat and eat and never gain weight. I'm trying to get away from meat as much as possible, to get away from cholesterol. I'm tempted quite often.

*What should your tombstone say?*

"He never met a food he did not like."

*What would your last meal be?*

You mean, before I went to the electric chair? My last request would probably be pumpkin pie made by my wife. She doesn't burn it: I like it kinda half baked.

*Like you?*

Yeah.

## JOE'S FATHER'S TOMATO SAUCE

*"Serve over your favorite pasta," says Ava Arpaio. "We like rigatoni or plain spaghetti."*

2 tablespoons olive oil
1 teaspoon garlic salt
1 pound ground beef
1 teaspoon Durkee Italian seasoning
1 (28-ounce) can tomato purée
1 (8-ounce) can tomato sauce
1 tablespoon sugar
1 teaspoon salt
1/4 teaspoon pepper

*In a medium-size skillet, sauté the garlic salt in olive oil on medium heat until golden. Add the ground beef, stirring the meat apart as it sautés. Stir in the Italian seasoning and cook 15 minutes. Drain and mix in the tomato purée, tomato sauce, sugar, salt, and pepper. Simmer, covered, for 1 hour or longer. Stir sauce occasionally while simmering. Serves 4 to 6.*

# Eddie Basha

*Grocer Eddie Basha is an Arizona native, and grew up in Chandler. His grandparents opened a general store in Ray in 1910, two years before statehood. From that store came the Bashas'*

*grocery chain, where he has worked since graduating from Stanford University. He was named president of Bashas' in 1968, which now has ninety stores statewide and is the only family-owned supermarket chain in Arizona.*

*A longtime advocate for children and education, he serves on the Arizona Board of Regents, and was a thirteen-year member of the Chandler School Board. He served on the State Board of Education for eight years, and was the Democratic candidate for governor in 1995.*

*Eddie Basha lives in east Chandler with his wife, Nadine Mathis Basha, and their two sons. He has three grown sons as well.*

*What did you eat when you were a child?*

I grew up with my mother, father, and grandmother, Najeeby. We called her "Jeeby." There was my Uncle Ike, four aunts, and me. Usually Jeeby was the cook. We were of meager means. She could take a leg of lamb and feed the family on it all week. We're Lebanese and we love to eat lamb, stuffed grape leaves, and cabbage rolls. Jeeby was a great cook, and to this day, my mother is a superb cook, too.

*What did you first cook?*

I remember making menudo with my dad when I was twelve or fourteen. My job was washing the tripe over and over before we cooked it in big cauldrons.

*What do you eat now?*

Once in a while my wife and I make Spanish rice, or salsa with some fresh baked tomatoes, fresh roasted chiles, a little onion, and a little oil. I also love to make salad—the traditional, prosaic salad with cucumbers, tomatoes, avocados, fresh mint, and romaine. I raise hell at the stores if the romaine isn't fresh. For the dressing, I mash some garlic cloves in olive oil, and add a little balsamic vinegar. My favorite meal is a broiled New York steak, baked potato, and salad.

*Ever have any cooking disasters?*

I once almost served a turkey that wasn't done. The oven wasn't set properly. Thank God I didn't have a bunch of people over at the time.

*What's your downfall?*

Ice cream. Bashas', of course. Made by Shamrock. Chocolate Chocolate. I dream about chocolate. It's a real addiction.

*Where do you like to eat in the Valley?*

Vincent's, Morton's Steakhouse, China Doll, and Serrano's Mexican Food. I love Italian food, especially Avanti's and Marcella's.

*Any foods you hate?*

Gimme a break. I never met a plate of food I didn't like.

## COOSA AND SAUTÉED ZUCCHINI

2 (6–8-ounce) rib steaks
  (or shoulder of lamb), fat
  removed and coarsely ground
¾ cup white rice
1 heaping teaspoon salt
¼ teaspoon cinnamon
12 medium zucchini squash,
  washed, halved, centers
  removed and set aside
1 teaspoon salt dissolved in
  1 quart cold water
Salt and pepper to taste
1 (12–16-ounce) hunk of ribs, or
  beef or lamb bones
1 (28-ounce) can stewed tomatoes
1 (11½-ounce) can tomato juice
½ cup chopped onion
1 tablespoon olive oil
1 (4-ounce) can diced green chiles
2 medium tomatoes, chopped
seasonings of your choice, to taste
¾ cup grated cheese of
  your choice

*Wash the ground beef in cold water. Mix with the rice, salt, and cinnamon.*

*Wash the cored zucchini in the salt/water mixture and stuff with the meat/rice mixture.*

*Lightly salt and pepper the ribs and place them on top of a rack in the bottom of a large pot. Pack the stuffed zucchinis on their ends on top of the ribs. Pour the stewed tomatoes and the tomato juice on top. Cover and bring to a boil. Reduce the heat to medium and cook for 2 hours.*

*In a medium-size skillet, lightly sauté the zucchini centers with the chopped onion in the olive oil 5 minutes. Add the green chiles, chopped tomatoes, seasonings, and cheese. Stir and serve with the Coosa.*

*Serves 6.*

# The Bombeck Family

CLOCKWISE FROM TOP: ANDY, BETSY, AND MATT BOMBECK

*Erma and Bill Bombeck moved to the Valley from Bellbrook, Ohio, in 1971 so Bill could get his doctorate in education at Arizona State University. Erma was already a successful syndicated columnist covering what she called "the utility room beat," and the Bombeck children—Betsy, Andy, and Matt—were all teenagers. Among Erma's dozen or so popular and highly entertaining books are* The Grass is Always Greener over the Septic Tank *and, illustrated by Bil Keane,* Just Wait till You have Children of Your Own!, *(both Fawcett).*

*The family liked the Valley so much they stayed. Bill became Dr. Bill, Erma continued to write from her room office (on her IBM Selectric; she never went computer), and the kids grew up. Well, grew older, at any rate.*

*Sadly, Erma left us in early 1996, but her family lives on, and in fact, there's a new little Bombeck to brighten everyone's lives. Eva Louise Bombeck was born January 6, 1997, to Matt and Jackie Bombeck, Bill and Erma's son and his wife.*

*Erma's children continue to be just as strange and wonderful as she described them. Betsy and Andy live in Phoenix; she's in retail, and he teaches fourth grade. Matt and Jackie live in Santa Monica, California, where Matt writes scripts for television movies.*

---

*What did you grow up eating?*

**BETSY:** We ate what people ate in the Midwest. Chicken, potatoes, steak, hamburger, Jell-O. And liver—my mom would cook bacon to cover up the smell. She started to get creative in her cooking after we moved out here.

**MATT:** She became a really good cook after we left the house. Her cooking was functional when we were little, maybe because we didn't like anything she made.

**BETSY:** I wouldn't eat anything. The only vegetables I would eat were carrots and corn. I ate ketchup on everything, even my tuna fish sandwich.

*Did you cook as a child?*

**ANDY:** I remember making French toast for my parents on Mother's Day and Father's Day when I was about ten.

**BETSY:** Dad said it smelled like Andy was making rubber tires. I used to bake cookies all the time. I once made some French lace cookies that were so burned, they became like weapons.

*Any other cooking disasters?*

**BETSY:** One time Mom made about five gallons of gazpacho, which she froze and we ate for an entire year. Another time her Cherry Surprise didn't gel and we ended up having cherry soup.

*What was your most memorable meal?*

**BETSY:** Mine was going to Chasen's with my family years ago. I remember Mom having their chili, which was really good, and one of us having this huge seafood cocktail that had every kind of seafood coming out of it. It was totally fun.

**ANDY:** I remember when we were in Greece, and I was treating my parents to this place I'd picked out. Well, this restaurant had cats everywhere: under the tables, on the tables, hanging in the trees. Mom had this huge fear of cats so she started yelling at me. It was awful.

**MATT:** My mother looked like a pretzel, with her arms and legs wrapped all around her. It was the night from hell.

*What do you eat now?*

**MATT:** I'm not a great cook but I'm fast and I can improvise. Jackie doesn't cook but she cleans up. I actually like to cook but I hate cleaning up. I'll make pasta, or just whip something up from what's in the fridge. I get that ability to whip things up from my mom.

**BETSY:** Mom could do things fast. That's why she got so much done. Bam, there's a meal. I'm single so I don't cook much. I may barbecue a steak or have some cheese and crackers. When you don't have to report to anybody, you can have brie and French bread for dinner.

**ANDY:** I'll just bake a potato in the microwave and fry the heck out of some meat, maybe a hot dog. I have a lot of hot dogs in the freezer. I had a hot-dog stand in downtown Phoenix during my break from teaching school last summer. I thought it would be a great idea to make some money. But people don't want to buy hot dogs when it's 120 degrees outside. So I still have plenty of hot dogs.

*What are your favorite restaurants?*

**ANDY:** We've always gone to Avanti's; my mom loved their food.

**MATT:** She would eat snails there. Escargot is a nicer name but I call them snails. I don't eat them. We have snails on the sidewalk in California.

**BETSY:** We used to go to the Tee Pee, and my parents liked Vincent's. Also El Chorro—when it's beautiful weather, the patio is wonderful for brunch.

*What's your food philosophy?*

**ANDY:** Order as much as you can for as little as possible.

**BETSY:** If someone else is paying for it, order a steak. Always get dessert.

**MATT:** Don't eat with Andy. He has this awful habit of smelling his food.

## ERMA'S MOM'S STRAWBERRY DELIGHT

*A favorite birthday treat.*

1 (6-ounce) box strawberry Jell-O
2 cups boiling water, plus 1 cup cold
1 (12-ounce) box frozen strawberries, thawed and undrained
  (don't use fresh)
1 angel food cake, broken into
  small pieces
1 (16-ounce) tub Cool Whip,
  thawed

*In a medium-size bowl, mix the Jell-O with the hot water, then add the cold water. Add the strawberries and refrigerate until partly gelled. Pour into a 13 x 9-inch pan. Mix in the cake pieces. Top with the Cool Whip. Refrigerate 1 to 2 hours. Cut into squares.*
  *Serves 8 to 10.*

# am Campana

Scottsdale mayor Sam Kathryn Campana was raised in tiny Filer, Idaho. "My father delivered the rural mail route and my mother was the school librarian," she said. "It was a town of 800 so everybody knew your business, just like they do in a town of 175,000."

After college in Helena, Montana, Campana moved to Scottsdale at age twenty-one with a girlfriend, both of them "intending to teach in the Catholic schools." A summer job at Reuben's led to meeting and marrying attorney Richard Campana, with whom she "had a happily married life for a long time." Now single, she has three children: Cassidy, Katie, and Richie.

President of Arizonans for Cultural Development, Campana was named Arizona Arts Advocate of the Year in 1987. She was elected mayor in 1995.

**What did you eat growing up?**

We lived off the land. We ate the fish my brothers caught and the deer and pheasant they shot. We grew up eating vegetables out of a neighbor's garden, which we worked. My mother and I canned fruit for the winter. We ate in a restaurant maybe twice a year. Everybody lived that way there.

**Was your mother a good cook?**

She could make pheasant like you'd find in the finest restaurant. We used to laugh that you knew what day it was by what was for dinner. Monday was hash made from Sunday's leftover roast; Tuesday was spaghetti. Sunday nights we'd watch Ed Sullivan and Bonanza.

**When did you learn to cook?**

I was no chef but I knew how to cook the staples. Meat loaf, roast, fried chicken. When I grew up, the women cooked and cleaned; the men hunted and fished.

**Ever have any cooking disasters?**

Two, actually. When I was a newlywed and hosting both families for the first time, I decided to make prime rib because we loved the prime rib at The Other Place, so I ordered a twenty-rib roast from Carl's Meats. When I went to pick it up, it was about three feet long, and looked like the side of a horse. I remember the bill was $112, which was more than my food budget for an entire

month, but you couldn't just say, "never mind." Somehow I got it home and cooked it in shifts.

I cook very seldom now. My most recent disaster was last year when I invited several friends over, and then went to Scottsdale Farmer's Market on Sixty-eighth Street and got greens and every wonderful thing for a salad. I made some nice bread and cooked chicken breasts Cajun style. I have the biggest salad bowl in town, which I tossed this fabulous salad in, along with an olive-oil dressing. With the first bite, we found that the oil was rancid. We all got up and went to Tucchetti for dinner, and came back to my house for dessert.

**Have any favorite fast foods?**

Yogurt and a banana from Circle K.

**How about sinful foods?**

Marian Saba's baklava, Danny Harkins' popcorn (sometimes I stop by for it when I'm not going to the movies), and Cathy Bua's rum cakes. Most people think I've gone to the Thursday Art Walk the past thirteen years for the art, but it's Cathy's rum cake.

**Where do you like to dine out?**

Oh, so many places. Rancho Pinot Grill, Marco Polo, Tutto, Arcadia Farms, Baby Kay's, and Don & Charlie's. If I'm entertaining at home, I'll usually call Havana Cafe.

## SAM'S FRANGO MINT COOKIES

*"It's like a Mexican wedding cookie but with a surprise."*

1 cup (2 sticks) margarine, softened
½ cup powdered sugar, plus some to roll cookies in
1 teaspoon vanilla extract
2¼ cups flour
¼ teaspoon salt
1 cup chopped pecans (optional)
1 cup (½-pound box) Frango chocolate mints* or 24 Hershey's Kisses

*In a medium-size bowl, cream the margarine and 1/2 cup sugar, and add the vanilla.*

*In a small bowl, combine the flour and salt and add to the margarine/sugar mixture, mixing well into a stiff dough. Mix in pecans. Refrigerate for 2 hours.*

*Preheat oven to 325°F.*

*Wrap 1 tablespoon of dough around each Frango mint, taking care to seal entirely, and place on a greased cookie sheet. Bake for 20 minutes. Cool thoroughly on racks, then roll in powdered sugar.*

*Makes 24 cookies.*

*Frango mints are available by mail-order at 1-800-5-FRANGO.

# len Campbell

Glen Campbell grew up in rural Arkansas, one of twelve children. He started his musical career as a studio musician who couldn't read music but sang backup for Frank Sinatra, Ray Charles, and Nat King Cole, then launched a solo career in the '60s and '70s with such hits as "Wichita Lineman," "Gentle on My Mind," and "By the Time I Get to Phoenix." He has ten gold albums, fourteen gold singles, and four Grammy awards. His recent autobiography, Rhinestone Cowboy, sold more than 150,000 copies.

An Arizona resident since 1981, Campbell lives in the Arizona Biltmore area with his wife, Kim, and children, Cal, 14; Shanon, 12; and Ashley, 10. He has five children from previous marriages, and five grandchildren.

**What did you eat, growing up?**

If Mama cooked it, we ate it. Chicken, squirrel, eel, gar, possum. Daddy would shoot about fifteen to twenty squirrels, and we'd eat squirrel for a week.

**How poor were you?**

We were so poor we couldn't afford laxatives. Our folks would set us on the pot and tell us ghost stories.

**What's your favorite food now?**

Fish; I like any kind that swims, especially salmon and sea bass. And the country stuff: roast chicken, pork chops, biscuits and gravy, mashed potatoes. Chili.

**Is your wife a good cook?**

I wouldn't say she's a bad cook, but a swarm of flies got together and fixed the screen door. She uses the smoke alarm for a timer. [Questioned, Campbell admits these are old Roger Miller jokes.] Actually, Kim's a good cook.

**Are you careful what you eat?**

I'm lucky that I've never had to watch it. I weigh around 188 or 189 pounds all the time. Not bad, considering I'm four foot two.

**Where do you like to eat?**

Don & Charlie's. Tomaso's. And P. F. Chang's is awesome. I had their leftover orange peel chicken and shrimp fried rice for lunch today. We go to Garcia's some, but I don't like Mexican food; I had plenty of beans when I was little.

**What's your favorite fast food?**

The chicken sandwich at McDonald's. Or whatever's left over.

**Remember any all-time peak dining experiences?**

One time in the Governor's Mansion in Arkansas when Winthrop Rockefeller was governor, my mama and daddy were there with us, and we had the best prime rib au jus I've ever had. I thought, boy, if all politicians ate like this, no wonder we're in trouble.

**What would your last meal be?**

Really good down-home cooking. Deep-fried pork chops, black-eyed peas, mashed potatoes. Bud Glaze's wife's homemade peanut brittle. She makes the best peanut brittle in the world.

### GLEN CAMPBELL'S FAVORITE CHILI

½ pound dry pinto beans
3 green bell peppers, seeded and coarsely chopped
3 large (1½ pounds) onions, coarsely chopped
2 cloves garlic, crushed
½ cup minced fresh parsley
1½ tablespoons olive oil
2½ pounds ground beef (medium priced)
1 pound lean ground pork
½ cup chili powder
2 tablespoons salt
1½ teaspoon ground pepper
1½ teaspoon ground cumin
3 (28-ounce) cans whole peeled tomatoes, undrained

*Soak the beans overnight (uncovered, unrefrigerated) in cold water. Drain, rinse, and cover the beans with fresh cold water and simmer in a large saucepan for 2 hours. ("Pouring out the water and rinsing the beans reduces gas effects.")*

*In a large skillet, sauté the green pepper, onion, garlic, and parsley in the olive oil. Add the ground beef and pork. Brown, and add the chili powder, salt, pepper, cumin, and tomatoes. Cook for 10 minutes over low heat. Add to the beans, cover, and cook for 1 hour.*

*Uncover and cook for another 30 minutes, adding water if needed.*

*Makes 4 quarts; serves 8.*

# Michael Carbajal

Inspired by Roberto Duran, fighter Michael Carbajal wanted to box from the time he was six years old. He began sparring at fourteen, managed by his brother, Danny Carbajal, whose nickname for Michael was "Little Hands of Stone." Within seven years, Carbajal took the Silver Medal at the 1988 Olympics in Seoul, Korea.

Since going professional, he has won $6.5 million and has the distinction of never being knocked out; he has been off his feet only twice in forty-seven bouts. In January 1997 he collected $150,000 for the tenth-round knockout of Scott Olson in Corpus Christi.

The longtime International Boxing Federation junior-flyweight champion was born in Phoenix and continues to live there, with his wife, Merci, and children: Erica, Michelangelo, Daniella, Mikito, and Micaela.

*What did you grow up eating?*

Rice, beans, and tortillas. My mom would cook Mexican food all the time.

*Did you cook anything?*

I didn't have to. If I got hungry and my mom wasn't cooking, I'd just eat some cereal.

*Ever have any cooking disasters?*

I left some rice on and forgot all about it. Oh, man, that pan burned. I had to throw it away.

*What do you like to eat now?*

Mainly fish. Seviche or Siete Mares, soup with clams, octopus, fish, a little tomato, a little cabbage, and some fresh jalapeño. I'm in training all the time, so seafood and pasta is about it. I eat a whole lot, but not heavy foods.

*What restaurants do you like?*

Sometimes we go to Tacos de Juarez, San Carlos Bay, the Olive Garden, Thai Rama, or DaVang, but mostly we eat at home. I like Merci's cooking better than anybody's. There is one restaurant I want to try, though. P. F. Chang's. I hear a lot about it. I'm going there sometime.

*Do you like sweets?*

Oh, yeah. My favorite is cheesecake. I like any cheesecake. Give me a cheesecake and I eat it. I even eat cheesecake from Jack in the Box.

## MERCI'S TORTILLAS

*"These are kind of a pain-in-the-butt to make," says Merci Carbajal, "but they're worth it. When Michael's not training, they're gone in two or three days."*

4 cups all-purpose flour, plus ¼ cup for working dough
1½ teaspoons salt
½ teaspoon baking powder
4 tablespoons Morrell's Snow-cap lard, room temperature
1¼ cups water

*Heat a griddle to medium-low. Mix the flour, salt, and baking powder in a large bowl. Add the lard and mix by hand. Sprinkle water over the dough, kneading until it has elasticity.*

*Form dough balls about 2 inches in diameter. Dip them into a bowl that has 1/4 flour in it, and flatten by hand into a circle. Roll out thin with a rolling pin, and stretch larger by hand before placing on the griddle.*

*Cook the tortillas until bubbles form on the first side; flip and cook the other side briefly. Keep the cooked tortillas covered in a towel while you're cooking the remaining tortillas.*

*Makes 2 dozen.*

# Carol Cavazos

Carol Cavazos, KPHO Channel 5's evening news anchor, grew up in Shaumberg, Illinois, and earned her degree in print journalism from the University of Houston. She left Chicago for Texas "after that third blizzard in a row, the kind where all you see of your car is the antenna."

Following ten years in Houston and San Antonio, Cavazos moved to Phoenix in January 1995. She has lived through several summers here, and claims to "love the dry heat."

Here, she's captured during a hang-gliding lesson.

*What did you eat as a child?*

Steak and potatoes. Chicken. Corned beef. Tacos. My mother worked but she cooked for us every single night, or my dad would barbecue.

*When did you begin cooking?*

I'd help get things started from the time I was in the fifth grade. My brothers and I took turns doing the dishes, too. One time my brother had left this huge pan full of grease on so I decided to cook that baby while I sat and watched cartoons. One of my brothers went in the kitchen and saw the pan smoking. "You're going to get in trouble," he said. We decided to throw water on it and that's when the flames roared across the ceiling over our heads. Then the flame went out. But I did get in trouble. My dad had to paint the ceiling.

*Did you hate any food?*

Liver. But maybe that's because my mother cooked the heck out of it. I guess she wanted to make sure all the germs were killed.

*How about now—what fast foods do you like?*

At home, I'm one of those Lean Cuisine/Healthy Choice–type people. Or I'll go out for a hot dog from Luke's.

It's the best Chicago-style dog with that fluorescent-green relish. And I'd be remiss if I didn't say McDonald's; my mom works for their corporate office. So McDonald's is one of my favorites.

*Any special dining-out places you like?*

For me, it's not just the meal, it's the whole experience. I love a view, whether it's the top of the John Hancock Building in Chicago, or Louie's on the Lake around the NASA area in Houston, or Windows on the Green here at The Phoenician. I also like La Locanda, a little Italian place near where I live.

*When you're eating healthy, what do you go for?*

Broccoli, beets, spinach. And bananas; I'll typically bring a couple bananas to work.

*What's your favorite sinful food?*

Chocolate, chocolate, chocolate! I lift weights, do fifty sit-ups, one hundred squats, and ride five miles on my stationary bike three times a week, so I can have chocolate.

## GUACAMOLE

2 ripe avocados, mashed
2 small ripe Roma tomatoes, chopped
⅓ cup chopped cilantro
2 tablespoons minced onion
1 clove garlic, minced
1 jalapeño, minced (optional)
Juice of 1 lemon
(about 3 tablespoons)
½ teaspoon salt

*Mix all ingredients and serve within a half hour "so it doesn't get that funny color." Serve with tortilla chips. Serves 4.*

# Anne Coe

Painter Anne Coe, known for her playful renditions of Southwestern flora, fauna, and food, lives near Apache Junction with her husband, Robert "Bronco" Horvath, her pet wolf, Virginia Woolf, and her dog, Woody.

She is the illustrator of Here's the Southwestern Desert, *published in 1995 by Disney-owned Hyperion Books. She exhibits her fine art at Joy Tash Gallery in Scottsdale. Several of Coe's recent paintings deal with gluttony, her* "favorite of the seven deadly sins."

*A fourth-generation Arizonan, Coe grew up on a farm at Wellton and at every meal ate meat:* "mostly beef. That was just the way you ate then."

*When did you learn to cook?*

I was pretty little when I'd help my grandmother snap beans, and watch her squeeze those little edges on pies. Later, when I was in the seventh grade, I made fudge that didn't harden, and my boyfriend was horrified. I remember being appalled and thinking, "This guy's a jerk."

*You're quite an adventurous cook now. How'd that come about?*

Your whole perception of food changes when you travel. I was a flight attendant for Western in the 1970s, and later, a group of us lived in Puerto Rico, where we started a gourmet club. We could fly to St. Thomas for wines and French products. We'd have these thirteen-course meals. Food became the center of my life.

*Do you cook much now?*

All the time. I've built my house with everything radiating out from the kitchen. Basically, we are into very light, healthy cooking—soups, vegetables. My husband makes a great lasagna. We don't cook meat, but I will eat whatever is served to me.

*Have any favorite fast foods?*

Wendy's. They have real ketchup. You don't have to rip open those little deals. Sometimes I just have to have a hamburger. I am an American, after all!

*Where do you like to eat out?*

RoxSand's. I also like The Farm at South Mountain and restaurants run by individuals. I'm sick to death of chains. At The Pleasures of the Palette (an annual spring art auction benefiting the Center Against Sexual Assault), I had something I thought of for weeks afterward. Made by Drew Nieporent, the chef at Tribeca Grill in New York, it was a salmon filet encrusted with truffles: You cut into this soft, moist, slightly pink salmon that was luscious.

*What's your favorite sinful food?*

Chocolate. I'm a chocoholic. I gave it up about two years ago and lost twenty pounds.

*Any foods you hate?*

Liver. And I don't eat veal. It's a political thing.

*If you were a chef, what kind would you be?*

I'd be like RoxSand. Magic realism. She's the Isabel Allende of the culinary world, and I like to think of myself as the Isabel Allende of art.

*What should your tombstone say?*

"She's just part of the food chain now."

## ANNE COE'S UNEXPECTED—COMPANY BLACK BEAN CAKES

*"This recipe welcomes experimentation. Try the bean cakes with grated cheese, sliced olives, chiles, etc. They're great on corn chips and make a really great hors d'oeuvres."*

2 (15½-ounce) cans black beans, drained and mashed (or use your own recipe made from dried beans)
1 teaspoon chili powder
1 teaspoon garlic powder
1 teaspoon unsweetened cocoa
2–3 tablespoons olive oil
¾ cup sour cream
1 small bunch fresh cilantro

*Mix the beans, chili powder, garlic powder, and cocoa in a large bowl and form into small pancakes. Heat the oil over medium low in a medium-size skillet. Fry cakes on both sides until crisp. Top each cake with a dollop of sour cream and a few sprigs of cilantro.*
*Serves 6.*

# Jerry Colangelo

Phoenix Suns president and CEO Jerry Colangelo is the godfather of Arizona sports, and arguably the prime architect of downtown Phoenix.

A Chicago boy who grew up in the Hungry Hill neighborhood, he played basketball and baseball in high school, and went on to attend the University of Illinois, where he earned All–Big Ten honors. He was later inducted into the Illinois Basketball Hall of Fame. He began his sports management career with the Chicago Bulls, and came to Phoenix in 1968 as the Suns' first general manager. Then twenty-eight, he was the youngest GM in pro sports.

A thirty-one-year veteran of the NBA, Colangelo led a group that purchased the Suns for $44.5 million. Under his leadership, the America West Arena became the centerpiece for the downtown revitalization, which now includes the Bank One Ballpark. His efforts to bring major-league baseball and professional hockey to Arizona came to fruition in 1995 with the Arizona Diamondbacks and the Phoenix Coyotes, now playing in the Valley.

He and his wife, Joan, have four children and six grandchildren.

*What did you eat growing up?*

Italian food, of course. Most everyone in our neighborhood was from the old country. They had their little gardens out back, or in any empty space around. There was a bakery a block away from our house, and the whole neighborhood had this great aroma. To me, a king's meal was some fresh Italian bread with Italian salami, mortadella, and capacolla. And tomatoes: I used to keep a salt shaker in my back pocket for the times when we were out playing ball and I'd pick a tomato out of a garden.

My grandfather made a little wine in the basement, and my mother would make pasta fagioli, gnocchi, or ravioli. I may be prejudiced but I think hers is the best ravioli anywhere. And her pizzelles? The best.

*When did you first cook?*

I'm very limited. Pasta is an easy thing, and I like to cook fresh Italian sausage out on the grill. I still have friends who send sausage to me from Chicago. My wife cooks mostly; she makes a great fresh sauce with tomatoes, garlic, and oil.

*Ever have any cooking disasters?*

Oh, yes. Many years ago, we had just put in a pool and grill at our house in Moon Valley, and we had thirty to forty people over for dinner. I was grilling, and I burned up all the lamb chops.

*What restaurants do you like?*

Pizzeria Bianco is my favorite. And I have to have my P. F. Chang's fix once in a while. I like Tomaso's, Christopher's, the Tee Pee, Ruth's Chris, and La Piñata.

*What are your favorite sinful foods?*

Unfortunately, I still like my chocolate. Especially malts. Johnny Rocket's makes a great one.

## MOM'S PIZZELLES

1 dozen eggs, room temperature
4 teaspoons vanilla extract
1 (1-ounce) bottle anise extract
1 (1-ounce) jar anise seed
1 pound (4 sticks) margarine
3 cups sugar
6 cups flour
6 teaspoons baking powder
1 orange peel, grated (1 to 2 tablespoons)

*Beat the eggs in a medium-size bowl until frothy. Add the vanilla, anise extract, and anise seed. Mix and set aside.*

*Melt the margarine in a medium-size saucepan, and add the sugar. Stir thoroughly and set aside to cool.*

*In a large bowl, combine the flour and baking powder. Add the grated orange peel. Blend in the egg and margarine mixtures; stir well.*

*Preheat a pizzelle iron. Place 1 teaspoon of batter on the iron and bake until light brown. Cool cooked pizzelles on paper towels. Store in a tightly covered (not plastic) container.*

*Makes 80 to 100 cookies.*

# Ike Cole

If the velvety voice of the man at the Arizona Biltmore piano sounds familiar, especially on songs like "Route 66" and "Ramblin' Rose," it's because the singer is the brother of the legendary Nat King Cole.

Born in Chicago, Isaac Cole was the fourth of five children, just younger than Nathaniel. "Dad was a Baptist minister, and Mom directed the church choir. All of us began playing the piano and participating in church." The family moved to Waukegan, and young Cole joined the army, playing for the 327th Army Band. After he got out, he formed a weekend trio, going on the road in 1957, during the time that Nat Cole was making a name for himself recording his mega hits.

Ike Cole played piano for "Route 66"

on the Unforgettable *album, which includes Natalie Cole's 1993 hit duo recorded with her late father's voice.*

*A Phoenix resident since 1986, Ike Cole now plays Sunday brunch at the Arizona Biltmore, and Tuesday evenings at J. Chew's in Scottsdale. He lives with his wife, Margie, in the Sun Lakes area of Chandler.*

*What did you eat as a child?*

Dad loved chicken so we had it any kind of way it could be cooked. And Mom made great spaghetti, liver, pork chops, roasts, and the best rolls in the world.

*What do you like to eat now?*

Oh, sole, salmon, catfish, spaghetti and meatballs. Pinto beans, rice, shrimp, all kinds of beef, and pork roasts. We don't eat out that often. My wife does the whole thing. She's a good cook.

*Like any sinful foods?*

I like breakfast rolls. German chocolate cake. The Biltmore's cheesecake. But I don't eat any of that too often.

*What was your peak dining experience?*

When I was in Baltimore in 1947 in the army, Nat was playing at the Paramount Theater for six weeks, and the next year at the Zanzibar. I went down there to be with him, and that was the first time I had a piece of that big ol' New York cheesecake. I've loved it ever since.

*What is your pet peeve regarding food?*

When I order food one way, and it comes another way. I send it back about half the time. Another problem is, if there's any rock, glass, or bug to be found, seems like it always winds up in my plate. One time in Milwaukee, I had one of those little bitty green worms on my salad. I called the waiter over and showed him, and he said, "Oh, he won't eat much." I didn't order another salad because he probably would have taken it to the kitchen, flicked it off, and brought the same salad back to me.

*What should your tombstone say?*

"If he loved it, he ate it."

## THE ARIZONA BILTMORE CHEESECAKE
*From Executive Chef Geoffrey Cousineau.*

*Serve it plain or with strawberry sauce. "I like it either way," says Cole.*

**CHEESECAKE:**
1 cup sugar
4 (8-ounce) packages cream cheese
1 teaspoon lemon zest
6 eggs
1 teaspoon vanilla extract
½ cup heavy cream
1 (10-inch) graham cracker crust

**STRAWBERRY SAUCE:**
1 quart strawberries, cleaned, and stemmed, and sliced
Juice of 1 lemon (about 3 tablespoons)
½ cup sugar

*Preheat the oven to 325°F.*
*To make the cheesecake, cream the sugar, cream cheese, and lemon zest in a large mixing bowl. Gradually add the eggs and the vanilla extract while mixing. Mix in the cream. Blend well.*
*Pour the mixture into the crust and place the pie pan into a larger pan with enough water to immerse pie pan one inch. Bake for 2 hours. Let the cake cool completely before removing from the pan.*
*Purée half the strawberries with the lemon juice in a food processor or blender. Add the sugar and fold in the remaining berries. Chill for 1 hour. Top cheesecake with 2 heaping tablespoons per slice.*
*Serves 12.*

# Sheryl Cooper

Dancer Sheryl Cooper met Alice Cooper in 1975 when she joined his "Welcome to My Nightmare" tour. She married the 1970s rock sensation the following year, and the two now live in Phoenix with their children; Calico, fifteen; Dash, eleven; and Sonora, four.

Known locally for her annual production of Hopi Elementary School's student talent show, Cooper is active in fund-raising events as well. She helps produce the Alice Cooper Celebrity Golf Tournament funding the Solid Rock Foundation, which establishes after-school centers for teens. Last held in February 1997 at the Arizona Biltmore, the event netted $125,000.

SHERYL AND ALICE COOPER AT THE FIRST ACCG GALA IN FEBRUARY 1997

Courtesy of Sheryl Cooper

*What did you think of Alice when you met him?*

I had never heard of him; I thought Alice Cooper was some blond folksinger. I knew Rachmaninoff but not rock. It took three other dancers to convince me to audition for his show. But I was one of two dancers hired out of the two thousand who auditioned.

I've done every one of the tours, and have had some real challenges. I've been a giant tap-dancing tooth, I've been a fluorescent dancing skeleton, and I've been a giant black spider in a sixty-foot hydraulic net. That's what I've done for love.

*What did you eat as a child, and what do you eat now?*

I remember big Sunday dinners while growing up. I still beat myself up for not making my grandmother write down her recipe for chicken and dumplings. Now, we tend toward pastas, salads, and grilling. Alice's manager, Shep Gordon, manages the great chefs of the world— people like Paul Bocuse and Michel Gerard—so I'm always gleaning little hints from them.

*Ever have any cooking disasters?*

Oh, yes. One time I put chicken livers in the lasagna. My brother-in-law, who is Italian, told me his mother did that.

Our guests were trying to be discreet while spitting it out into their napkins. It was vile.

*What's your peak dining experience?*

It was in Antwerp, Belgium. We celebrated our third anniversary in the Marlene Dietrich suite at the Rousseline Hotel, which had a giant four-poster you had to take a giant leap to get into. We filled the enormous gold bathtub with bubbles to our chin, and had chateaubriand from room service while one waiter threw rose petals into the tub, and another guy played the violin.

*What Phoenix restaurants do you like?*

Tarbell's, Eddie's Grill, Ayako, and we love P. F. Chang's: you cannot have a bad dish there. We like simple things. We don't go out a lot. The plates some restaurants serve are so ornate, you don't know whether to eat it or wear it.

*How about sinful foods?*

Neither of us indulges much. Alice runs every night when he's in training for a tour. But when I'm the slightest bit down, he'll slip me some M&Ms. I read an alarming statistic that it takes a walk across a football field to work off one M&M. I try not to get the slightest bit down.

## CHICKEN SALAD

*"Alice loves this. Everyone does."*

1 tablespoon butter
2 (2-ounce) packages slivered almonds
½ cup sugar
1 bunch scallions, including tops, minced (about ⅓ cup)
2 cups halved green grapes
½ cup low-fat mayonnaise
6 mesquite-grilled chicken breasts, sliced lengthwise into ½-inch strips

*Melt the butter in a large skillet over medium heat. Pour in the almonds and coat them with the butter. Add the sugar slowly, while stirring. Cook until golden brown and sizzling. Remove from the heat and combine with the scallions, grapes, mayonnaise, and chicken strips. Serve immediately or chill for later.*
*Serves 6.*

# Lattie Coor

Dr. Lattie F. Coor Jr., president of ASU, grew up in Avondale, the son of prominent schoolteachers. (Lattie Coor Elementary School in Avondale is named for his father, who graduated from ASU and was a member of the 1928 Bulldogs football team.) He graduated with honors from NAU in 1958. Coor and his wife,

Elva, built a rambling contemporary home on South Mountain in 1995, where they now enjoy a panorama of mountain views, from the White Tanks and the Bradshaws to the McDowells, with downtown Phoenix high-rises the central focus.

Both Coors are Arizona natives—

Elva part of the northern Arizona Wingfield clan, and Lattie's grandfather having settled at Eleventh Avenue and Baseline in 1909.

---

*What did you eat as a boy?*

We had a dairy cow, we grew vegetables, we had fruit trees, and we slaughtered our cattle. During hunting season we shot deer and elk. I first hunted deer at age seven or eight, and I shot my first elk on Mingus Mountain when I was twelve. I went hunting with some uncles who lived in Jerome [Arizona].

*Remember what you first cooked?*

Oh, yes. Dutch-oven biscuits. My parents were teachers, and after attending summer school in Greeley, Colorado, they'd take us camping in Colorado or in Yellowstone Park. I learned Dutch-oven cooking pretty young. Still love to cook that way. My specialty is Dutch-oven cobblers with fresh fruit and a little tapioca. Peaches are the best.

*Did you ever have any cooking disasters?*

Absolutely. One time I hosted a dinner where the centerpiece was to be a Greek salad. I had fallen in love with feta cheese, but when I stopped to pick it up, I mispronounced it and they gave me phyllo dough instead. I substituted Monterey Jack, but it wasn't the same.

*What's your favorite sinful food?*

Steak, no question. I like to grill it, preferably over hickory or oak. I'm not a chocoholic but I like a rich brownie with ice cream, and I can fall for pecan pie.

*Any foods you hate?*

I'm not big on cooked turnips.

*Where do you like to eat out?*

Los Dos Molinos, hands down.

*Elva told me that you like your food hot, and that she carries Tabasco in her purse for you. Do you cook with chiles?*

Very often. I developed a passion for chiles when I lived in Vermont. Now I make up several sauces using chiles, especially poblanos and pepitos.

## LATTIE'S CHILE PASTE

*"Brush this over ribs, chicken, roast, or game, and bake or grill over coals."*

6 dried ancho chiles
8 cloves garlic, unpeeled
½ cup peanut or olive oil, plus extra for adding to paste
salt and freshly ground black pepper to taste
1 chipotle chile (a canned smoked jalapeño)
2 teaspoons Dijon mustard
2 tablespoons red wine vinegar
¼ cup fresh sage leaves (or ⅛ cup dried rubbed sage)
¼ cup minced red onion

*Pour boiling water over the ancho chiles and allow them to sit until fully hydrated, at least 1 hour. Place the garlic cloves in a small glass dish. Pour 1 tablespoon of the oil over the garlic; sprinkle with salt and pepper. Place the garlic mixture in the microwave and cook for 10 seconds. Peel the cloves by squeezing the root end. (When cooked through but still firm, the clove will easily pop out of its peel.)*

*Drain the ancho chiles. Place all the ingredients in a food processor or blender and blend to a smooth paste, adding more oil if necessary.*

*After brushing on meat, remaining paste can be thinned with oil or water to use as a sauce for serving.*

*Makes one cup.*

*Vary this recipe by adding fresh rosemary, or by using tarragon or cilantro instead of sage. Cumin can be added in place of mustard and sage. Try mixing ancho chiles with pasilla, Anaheim, or other chiles. For hotter paste, add habanero or more chipotle. Keep the paste, covered, in the refrigerator for stir-fry, soups, and stews. Keeps three weeks.*

# Clive Cussler

Author Clive Cussler was an advertising man by day, and a novelist by night, until his Raise the Titanic! was published by Simon and Schuster and became a best-seller in 1975. Since then, he has sold more than 70 million books starring Dirk Pitt, an action hero loosely patterned on Cussler. "We're both about six-foot-three, and we're both addicted to the challenge of the search," he says. "His eyes are greener than mine, and he certainly enthralls the ladies more than I ever did."

Cussler was raised in Alhambra, California, where he "did all the crazy things kids did in the leisurely days before television, like jumping off the roof of a house under construction into a sand pile." He hated school, and barely managed to graduate ("I refused to do homework."). During college, he and a friend spent one summer driving around the country, covering thirty-six states. The entire trip cost him $350.

After serving in the air force during the Korean War, he returned to California, where he opened a service station with some friends, and later entered the advertising business.

Cussler and his wife, Barbara, have three children and two grandchildren. Since 1986, they have lived six months of the year in the Valley, where his many awards hang in his office bathroom.

*What did you eat as a child?*

You could tell what day it was by what we ate. Monday was stew, Tuesday was hash, Wednesday some awful pea soup, Thursday was liver and onions, Friday was chipped steak, Saturday was steak, and Sunday was chicken. But my favorite thing was a peanut-butter-and-mayonnaise sandwich with a big dill pickle. I wish I had a nickel for every fifty-five-gallon drum of peanut butter I've gone through. In fact, when we have all these gourmet meals while traveling in Europe, I'll sit there and dream of a peanut-butter sandwich.

*What did you first cook?*

A grilled-cheese sandwich, I guess. In high school, some friends and I took home ec and typing; it was a great way to meet girls since we were the only guys in the class. The girls would get mad at us because our cakes always rose higher than theirs.

*What do you like to eat now?*

Anything. I love to eat. I always cut out recipes and buy cookbooks.

*Are there any foods you hate?*

I'll eat anything, and have. I've had exotic things at the Explorers Club in New York. Eel, rhino, lion, zebra. I've never found any of them very good. The taste is usually blah or gamy.

*You're so prolific; do you write constantly?*

Oh, I'm not a dedicated writer like Stephen King and Mary Higgins Clark. I'll take a year or two off. And every year I spend two months on the sea. Plus, I spend a lot of time collecting cars. I have eighty cars in my warehouse in Colorado. Even have a 1929 Duesenberg and a 1948 Talbot-Lago sports coupe.

*What restaurants do you and Barbara like in Phoenix?*

We like The Other Place, Bistro Vagara, Vincent's, Havana Cafe, Avanti's, Steamers, RoxSand's, Piñon Grill, and The Phoenician for brunch. Their brunches are marvelous. I also like diners, especially old tacky ones like The Big Apple.

## CLIVE'S GUAVA-PRAWN SAUTÉ

6 tablespoons butter
2 cups fresh sliced guava (fresh mango or papaya can be substituted)
1½ pounds large prawns, shelled, deveined, and patted dry
¾ teaspoon salt
⅛ teaspoon freshly ground black pepper
¼ cup finely chopped mango chutney
2 tablespoons white wine vinegar
½ teaspoon dry mustard
⅛ teaspoon ground cloves
¾ cup chopped green onions, including tops
1 lime, cut into 8 wedges, for garnish

*Melt the butter in a large frying pan over medium heat. Add the fruit and the prawns just to coat with butter. Add the salt, pepper, chutney, vinegar, mustard, and cloves. Sauté, turning often, just until prawns are pink and firm, about 5 to 6 minutes. Add the onions and just heat through. Serve with the lime wedges. Serves 4 to 6.*

# Perry Damone

Perry Damone of KEZ Radio was famous even as a baby. The son of movie star Pier Angeli and singer Vic Damone (he was named for Perry Como), he grew up in his mother's native Italy, where he learned to speak Italian and French, and to cook.

At age twelve, he and his mother moved to Los Angeles, where he taught himself to speak English "by listening to radio, especially KHJ." He decided then that he wanted to be an announcer. "When I went to live with my dad after my mother died," he remembers, "I would put speakers into the air-conditioning ducts, and turn the whole house into a radio station."

After graduating from high school in Paris, and Richmond College in London, Damone began his career in broadcasting at KCOH in Houston.

*He has been at KEZ the past nine years, and lives in Fountain Hills with his wife, Nancy, who is also Italian.*

---

*When did you learn to cook?*

I made a pretty good sauce at six or seven, and was proficient at Caesar salad then, too. My mother and grandmother let me help with everything. I got to stand up on a chair.

*What'd you like best of your mom's cooking?*

Her sauce. Mmm. And she made a great rosemary chicken with lots of olive oil and fresh rosemary.

*What's your favorite sinful food?*

This is a nasty one. My sinful snack is prosciutto. I'll go through three-quarters of a pound in a week.

*Have a favorite healthful food?*

Sure, my healthful Caesar. The secret is Coleman's dry mustard. And fresh everything. And homemade garlic croutons.

*Do you cook at home?*

Almost every night. Steaks are on the barbecue right now, in fact. We back up to the McDowell Mountains and I can hear the coyotes howl when I'm barbecuing.

*Any foods you hate?*

I've been all over the world and have never run across a food I didn't like. From brains to sea urchins to octopus. My mother taught me how to catch sea urchins when we lived in Tuscany. We'd throw them into a steamer right on the boat and eat them then.

*What's your peak dining experience?*

I've peaked so many times. Here, I love La Fontanella. Berto and Isabella's Chicken Marsala is unbelievable, and they make their own gelato. It's like family there, with hugs and kisses.

*What should your tombstone say?*

"May he rest in pasta."

## SALSA DI NINA PIERO
(Nancy & Perry's sauce)

⅓ cup extra-virgin olive oil
2 large red onions, chopped
6 large cloves garlic, minced
1 (5-pound) pork tenderloin, deboned and tied
4 (28-ounce) cans whole peeled Roma tomatoes
2 (28-ounce) cans tomato sauce
1 (12-ounce) can tomato paste
2 cups water
2 bay leaves
2 teaspoons basil (optional)
1 tablespoon sugar
1 tablespoon red wine vinegar
salt and pepper to taste
16 ounces pasta

*Heat the oil in a large frying pan; add the onion and garlic. Sauté until tender, about 5 minutes. Brown the pork all over in the oil mixture. Add the remaining ingredients, except the pasta, to the pan. Simmer for 5 hours, covered, stirring every 15 minutes.*

*Cook the pasta.*

*Place the roast on a cutting board or platter; untie and slice. Arrange the slices over pasta, and cover with sauce.*

*Serves 8 to 10.*

# ent Dana

KPNX-TV news anchor Kent Dana is
a hometown boy. Born at Central and
Thomas, he was the third of seven kids.
"I still am, actually. That's the one
constant in my life," he says.

After getting his broadcasting degree
at BYU in 1971, Dana returned to
Phoenix and worked as a weekend radio
announcer for $3.50 an hour until he
could get a toehold in television at Tom
Chauncey's Channel 10.

Dana has been an award-winning
anchor at KPNX for sixteen years, and
he now co-hosts the evening news with
Jineane Ford.

Dana and his wife, Janet, are the
parents of six children, and live in
north Phoenix.

TAKING A BIG BITE OUT OF BREAKFAST IS
KENT DANA, WITH DAUGHTERS (LEFT TO
RIGHT): KELLY AND KARI.

*What did you eat growing up?*

Ours was a typical big family that didn't have a lot of money. My dad always fixed breakfast for us, usually oatmeal, and every Sunday my mother made roast beef and mashed potatoes. For every meal, my mother made sure we sat down at the table.

We hardly ever went out. A real treat was to go to the Carnation store on Central, and my parents would sometimes go to Jordan's, which was just down the street from our house. We lived at 37 West Edgemont. To this day, I love to go to Jordan's.

*Where else do you like to eat out?*

We like Macayo's, Valle Luna, P. F. Chang's, Los Compadres, and the Satisfied Frog. If we're in a very upscale, romantic mood, we love Avanti's. They don't pester you, but they don't ignore you.

*What's your favorite fast food?*

Burgers, pizza from Streets of New York, or I'll go pick up something from Boston Market.

*How about healthful food?*

Healthy food? I don't do it often so I have to really think about it. It's a constant battle because the camera adds ten pounds. My wife and I walk three miles four times a week, and we try to incorporate vegetables into what we eat.

*Any foods you hate?*

I don't like sushi; it tasted squirmy to me. It was kinda like: I don't need this in my mouth.

*What's your wife's cooking like?*

Excellent. She makes an unbelievably good ham loaf, and a lasagna that everyone says is the best they've ever had. She also makes a handed-down-through-the-family recipe for English toffee that's to die for. We'll give away forty to fifty boxes of it at Christmas. Every co-anchor I've ever had loves it.

*Do you cook?*

Not in a serious sense, but I can grill just about anything, and I make good shredded beef chimichangas.

*Ever have any cooking disasters?*

No, but one time my wife left the sugar out of pumpkin pie. You should have seen the look on everyone's face when they tasted it before she did.

## DORA'S HAM LOAF
*Dora is Kent Dana's mom.*

*"Everyone loves this," says Dana. "I like mine with a thin layer of horseradish sauce."*

**MEATLOAF:**
2 pounds ground pork shoulder
1 pound ground ham
1½ cups dry bread crumbs
2 eggs
1½ cups milk
1 teaspoon salt
½ teaspoon pepper

**GLAZE:**
½ cup brown sugar
1 teaspoon dry mustard
1 tablespoon freshly squeezed
   orange juice

*Preheat oven to 350°F.*
   *Combine all the meat loaf ingredients and shape into a meat-loaf pan. Bake for 1 hour.*
   *Mix the ingredients of the glaze and pour over the meat loaf. Bake another 15 minutes.*
   *Serves 6 to 8.*

# $\mathcal{R}$ita Davenport

Author/speaker Rita Davenport is one of the country's leading authorities on time management and motivation; she has addressed such groups as Xerox, AT&T, Honeywell, American Express, PepsiCo, and the National Security Council.

She grew up in Nashville, and earned her degree from Middle Tennessee State University. For fifteen years, she hosted a Phoenix television show, Cooking With Rita, and was seen in 32 million homes on her cable program, Success Strategies. She is president of Arbonne International, a direct sales/network marketing company.

Davenport has written four best-selling books, including Making Time, Making Money (St. Martin's Press), and De Grazia and Mexican Cookery (Northland Publishing). Her books have sold more than one million copies.

She and her husband, David Davenport, live in Paradise Valley with their sons, Michael, eighteen, and Scott, sixteen.

The final line of her introduction is usually, "She speaks two languages . . . English and Southern."

*What did you eat as a child?*

Anything that was fried or smothered in gravy. My mom was a great cook. She used to make great jam cake, fried chicken, vegetable soup, fresh apple cake and fresh coconut cake. Her popcorn balls were wonderful, and she made the best chocolate pie in the world. Everyone wanted to come to our house.

*When did you start cooking?*

I was raised poor, but we had real good Christmases. When I was six, I got a real electric stove for Christmas. I'm sure it would not pass UL underwriters today, but I remember cooking little tiny biscuits in it.

When I was in high school, I was an avid home ec student. One time another girl and I were partners in making a pie. Her responsibility was the dry ingredients, and mine was the liquid. She forgot the sugar. We ended up with this beautiful lemon meringue pie that nobody could eat. We passed it around to people we didn't like. One guy said you couldn't even get your lips apart after you ate it.

*Ever have any other disasters?*

I had a chef on the show doing a lobster dish one time. Well, he brought live lobsters and stabbed them with an ice pick, on camera. The calls we got! From then on, if someone said they were going to cook anything—even lamb—I'd make sure it was already dead.

And then there was Ralph Ammaccapane. [He is the grandfather of golfer Danielle Ammaccapane, featured on page 2.] The first time he came on, he was cute and funny, talking a mile a minute. The second time, he froze. The man's lip was quivering. He was just staring at the camera like a deer frozen in the headlights. Later on, he'd relaxed some but he'd forget he was on TV. He'd get excited and start cussing in Italian, or say a double entendre. I poked him in the ribs so much, he was bruised after my show. He was the best guest we ever had; men would come home at lunch time to watch Ralph.

*Are there any foods you can't stand?*

One thing Mama made that I hated was chitlins. Hog innards. I could smell them when I got off the school bus.

*What are your favorite sinful foods, and how do you eat them and stay trim?*

I'm famous for loving Goo-Goo Bars. I even got Bashas' to import them from Nashville, I talked about them so much. And I love chocolate cake, brownies, clove candy, and chocolate chip cookies. I used to tell Famous Amos that my cookies were better than his because I put a little coconut in them. He said, "You may make better cookies but I sell cookies better."

I can really put away the groceries. I try to run three to five miles a day on my treadmill to make up for what I eat.

*I can't help noticing you're wearing two watches, one of them a Rolex. Why?*

I wear this ten-dollar Timex because I can see it. I wear the eighteen-thousand-dollar Rolex because you can see it.

---

### RITA'S CHICKEN ENCHILADAS

1 (10¾-ounce) can cream-of-chicken soup
½ cup chicken broth
1 (4-ounce) can diced green chiles
¼ teaspoon pepper
2 tablespoons vegetable oil
6 corn tortillas
1 cup boned chicken
½ cup chopped onion
1 cup grated longhorn or cheddar cheese
½ cup sour cream (optional)

*Preheat oven to 375°F.*

*In a small bowl, mix together the soup, broth, chiles, and pepper. Set aside.*

*Heat the oil in a medium-size skillet over medium heat. Soften the tortillas by dipping them one at a time in the hot oil. Drain the tortillas on paper towels and stack.*

*Mix the chicken and onion in a small bowl. Put 2 tablespoons of the chicken mixture in the center of each tortilla. Sprinkle each with about 2 tablespoons of cheese and add dollops of sour cream, if desired. Roll the enchiladas and place them in a shallow baking dish.*

*Pour the soup mixture over the top and sprinkle with the remaining cheese. Bake 10 to 20 minutes.*

*Serves 3.*

(*From* De Grazia and Mexican Cookery, *Northland Publishing.*)

#  ugh Downs

*Hugh Downs, one of the best-known figures in broadcasting, grew up in Ohio, beginning his career as a radio announcer at the age of eighteen. "I was a teenage disc jockey but I didn't know it because the phrase hadn't yet been coined," he quips.*

*After a year of college followed by service in the U.S. Army, he joined NBC, and in 1957 helped launch* The Tonight Show *with Jack Paar, staying with the program for five years. "The show was so wild for its time. . . . Jack called me a walking encyclopedia because he'd turn to me for answers and I'd come up with something. My family took to calling me a " 'walking pamphlet.' "*

*Downs co-hosted NBC's* Today *show for many years, leaving in 1971 to*  *devote his time to teaching, lecturing, and writing. He is the author of seven books, including an autobiography,* Yours Truly, Hugh Downs, *(Holt, Rinehart & Winston). The recipient of two Emmy Awards, Downs is co-anchor of 20/20, ABC's weekly news magazine show, concentrating on science, medicine, aging, adventure, the arts, and family.*

*He and his wife, Ruth, live in Scottsdale and maintain a home in New York as well. They have two children and a grandson. Hugh, their son, "is a computer expert, and writes a lot of my radio commentaries. He thinks like I do," says Downs. Their daughter, Deirdre, is an artist living in Santa Fe. The Downs' grandson, Henry Young VI, twenty-seven, is an actor and director. He goes by Sadim.*

*What did you eat as a child?*

We lived for nine years on a farm near Lima, Ohio. It was the height of the Depression so we had no frills, but we were able to get by because we had this small farm. My dad didn't believe in bankruptcy and spent years paying off some debts. It was a mark of integrity I always admired.

We ate standard English fare. Chicken, ham, and bacon. Real strawberry shortcake with wild strawberries. I didn't understand gourmet; the condiments were salt and pepper. Once, my brother and I sold chickens at the roadside. We took turns killing them with a big double-bit ax. We were both proficient at this.

Our family bought day-old bread at a bakery. I remember that sliced bread came in when I was in my teens.

*Did you ever have any cooking disasters?*

Shortly after Ruth and I were married, I was doing the night shift at NBC in Chicago, and her birthday came around. I baked her a cake after getting off work, and when the recipe said to cream the sugar and butter, I thought it meant to add cream. I ended up making the whole thing all over again before the sun came up. It may not have won any blue ribbons, but Ruth had a nice marble cake.

*What do you eat now?*

Mostly fruits, grains, and lightly cooked vegetables. I'm very righteous, and then when my weight is where I want it to be, I take off and have a couple of martinis

and prime rib. I do like ostrich, too. It's delicious: tender like veal but with more character. However, if someone sees me putting my head in the sand, I'm obviously overdoing it.

*Ever eat fast foods?*

I hate to admit it but I like a Burger King, grilled, with a milkshake.

*Do you have cravings for sinful food?*

Yes, mostly in the dessert category. When you get down to it, my favorite all-time dessert is apple pie with vanilla ice cream. I must be American.

*What restaurants in the Valley do you like?*

There are many good eating places in Phoenix. A few we like are Tarbell's, Avanti's, Vincent's, The Grill at the Ritz Carlton, and around Carefree, where we used to live, Ianuzzi, the Satisfied Frog, the Horny Toad, and Rancho Mañana.

*A final question I have to ask. What is Barbara Walters really like?*

I resisted having her on the show, but she's been a real asset. I have always enjoyed working with her. She got a reputation early on for being acerbic, yet I have never seen her be unkind to a guest. She is hands-down the best interviewer. I think she got the reputation for being difficult from insecure males. Remember, she was the first woman in TV news to make over a million dollars a year.

## STUFFED ZUCCHINI

8 medium (6-inch) zucchini
1 tablespoon salt dissolved in a
    large bowl of water
1 heaping cup ground lamb
1 cup short-grained white rice, well
    washed and drained
1½ teaspoons plus a pinch of salt
¼ teaspoon pepper
¾ teaspoon cinnamon
2 tablespoons butter,
    room temperature
1 (6-ounce) can tomato paste
1 (16-ounce) can crushed tomatoes

*Wash the zucchini and cut off the stalk ends. Hollow out the interiors, taking care not to pierce the sides or ends of the squash. Place the cored zucchini in the salted water.*

*Combine the lamb, rice, 1½ teaspoons salt, pepper, cinnamon, butter, and a few spoonfuls of the tomato paste in a large bowl, mixing by hand.*

*Drain the zucchini. Fill each one with the lamb mixture, leaving one-third of space free for expansion during cooking. Place the stuffed zucchini in rows in a large pot. In a small bowl, mix the tomatoes and remaining paste, and pour over the squash. Add water to cover the zucchini and sprinkle with a pinch of salt.*

*Place a plate upside down on the top. Cover with the pot lid and cook on low heat about 1 hour or until the rice is done.*

*Serves 4.*

# Herb Drinkwater

Scottsdale mayor Herb Drinkwater grew up in Phoenix, the first of his family not born in England, he says. His father taught math at North High School, and Herb himself went to North, and then Phoenix College. A member of the Scottsdale City Council since 1970, he served as the city's mayor for fifteen years, retiring in 1995.

During his tenure, the area's private water companies were acquired by the city, a special tax was enacted to preserve the McDowell Mountains, and additional land was annexed, doubling Scottsdale's size to about 185 square miles. Led by Drinkwater, there was a successful drive to move the Phoenix Open to the Tournament Players Club. "It's the largest golf tournament in the world, with 400,000 paying participants," says Drinkwater. "And I'm not even a golfer!"

Drinkwater and his wife, Jackie, live in north Scottsdale in a home that overlooks Pinnacle Peak and nearby mountains. They have two children, Jamie Drinkwater Buchanan, a pharmacist, and Mark, a Scottsdale restaurateur, and two grandchildren, Bryce and Kelsie Buchanan.

*What did you eat as a child?*

My family all came from England, so every Sunday we had roast beef, oven-browned potatoes, Yorkshire pudding, and peas.

*When did you start to cook?*

I always liked to fool around in the kitchen. I cook over mesquite quite a bit at home. I'm a purist; I go out and cut my own mesquite. I like to cook whole prime ribs by smoking them slowly. I sometimes do that for fund-raising auctions.

  I'm an outdoor cook. I like to grill a five- or six-pound beef tenderloin with Montreal steak seasoning, cooking it about ten minutes on each side. Or I'll grill a leg of lamb after marinating it in wine, honey, vinegar, and fresh mint.

*Ever have any cooking disasters?*

Sure. I was probably ten or eleven when I was baby-sitting my sisters and brother one time, and decided to bake a cake. I put some red stuff in to make the batter darker, and instead of food dye, it turned out to be peppermint flavoring. The cake looked good but you couldn't eat it.

*What's your favorite fast food?*

I'm in a hurry all the time—I used to grab a burger but I ruined too many shirts and ties eating while driving, so now I stop and get a fresh fruit drink or yogurt.

*Have a favorite sinful food?*

Most of my food is sinful. I like all foods, and my favorite dessert is carrot cake. The city council is probably sick of carrot cake because they know that if we have a lunch somewhere, I'm going to make sure carrot cake's on our menu. The best carrot cakes I've had are at Hyatt Gainey Ranch, the Saguaro Cafe, 8700, and the Jamaican carrot cake made by Dorita Forbes.

*Where do you enjoy dining out?*

That's hard; Scottsdale has so many great places. I like Franco's Trattoria, Maria's When in Naples, Unbacio, Golden Swan, the Palm Court, Mulligan's, Avanti's, Jalapeños, Leland's, Latilla at the Boulders. We also love to go to Drink-water's at Pinnacle Peak and eat at the bar: Bill and Georgia Teich are the majority partners in it with Jackie and me. And I always find myself at Vincent's; I just wish he was in Scottsdale! I love his lamb, served with the smoking rosemary. One time when I was there with the police chief, we smelled that rosemary burning and I said, "Jeez, it's marijuana, you'll have to arrest him."

*What would your tombstone say?*

"Some people eat to live, he lived to eat."

## JACKIE DRINKWATER'S CHILI VERDE

*"Enjoy this with warm flour tortillas or over fresh tamales, topped with grated cheese, sour cream, and chopped green onions."*

1 large onion, chopped
3 tablespoons olive oil
2 pounds beef or pork, fat removed, cut into ½-inch cubes
2 cloves garlic, crushed
3 tablespoons red wine vinegar
1 (8-ounce) can tomato sauce
1 cup red wine
1 bay leaf
1 tablespoon oregano
1 (4-ounce) can diced green chiles
1 (17-ounce) can green chile salsa
salt and pepper to taste

*In a large frying pan, sauté the onion in 2 tablespoons of the oil for 3 to 5 minutes, stirring constantly. Remove the onion from the pan and set aside. Add the remaining 1 tablespoon of oil to the pan and brown the meat. Return the onion to the pan and add the remaining ingredients. Bring to a boil, reduce heat, and simmer, covered, until meat is fork-tender, about 1½ to 2 hours.*
  *Serves 8.*

# ex Earnhardt

Car dealer Tex Earnhardt was raised near the Mexican border in south Texas, where he quit high school to work in a tire store, and rodeo on weekends. He moved to Arizona in 1950, and shortly after began selling used cars in Chandler.

Now sixty-five, he and his sons, Hal and Jim Babe, are the highest-volume Jeep and Ford dealers in Arizona, and "the number-one Dodge dealer in the world," he says. "We spend a million dollars a month in advertising."

Earnhardt and his wife, Pam, live in Chandler, on the ranch he has owned for thirty-seven years.

*What did you eat growing up?*

Fried steak, fresh vegetables, hominy grits, iced tea, and beans. Every woman's always got 'em on her stove. Beans is a good thing. I eat 'em every day; I'm just used to beans. Put a little onion and salsa on 'em. Ain't nothing any better. Unless it's chicken-fried steak. Down there, they beat hell out of the steak and batter it in the same stuff you fry chicken in. Mmm. I'm gettin' hungry telling you all this.

*Was your mom a good cook?*

Phenomenal. She makes that southern food I like, all greasy. And she makes a Grapenuts pudding that's wonderful. I need some of that. Have to get her to make me some.

*What do you eat now?*

Anything and everything. Pam's an excellent cook. Everything she makes I like. Pastas. Salads. It's not fancy, just good food. She sets a pretty table, too.

*You like fast food?*

Oh, yeah. I eat 'em all, but Taco Bell's my favorite. I'll eat a dozen of their tacos.

*Where do you and Pam dine out?*

We'll go to Houston's when we come to town; they have awful good food. In Chandler, Moon Garden's a good Chinese place, and we go to the country club at Sun Lakes. But I'd usually rather stay home and eat a peanut-butter sandwich.

*What's your favorite sinful food?*

I don't know that there's any food that's not good for me. I don't put on weight. Only thing that's bad is if I eat late at night or eat too much; then I'm so full I can't lay down. I like sweets—donuts, cakes, bagels. One thing that's phenomenal are those Cathy's Rum Cakes that Cathy brings to our parties.

*Any foods you hate?*

There's nothing I will not eat. I've had sow bellies, cow eyeballs, rattlesnake meat, and armadillo; you know, armadillo is quite a delicacy.

## TEX'S MORNING OATMEAL

*Tex doesn't add milk, but if you do, "warm it up first," he says. "This is to die for. You don't even need to eat lunch if you have this for breakfast."*

1¾ cups water
1 cup thick-cut oatmeal (available at health food stores)
2 teaspoons vanilla extract
2 tablespoons brown sugar
1 teaspoon cinnamon
½ cup raisins
½ cup chopped walnuts

*Boil the water in a 1-quart saucepan. Add the oats, cooking 5 to 7 minutes, uncovered, on low heat. Stir in the remaining ingredients, and let the oatmeal sit for a minute or two before serving.*
*Serves 2.*

# Al Feinberg

Al Feinberg is "in reporter heaven" as the features reporter on Channel 15. "I've seen more than enough murder trials, hurricanes, and highway accidents in my twelve years in TV news," he says. His "Al's World," at the end of the newscast, "is your dessert, like eating all your vegetables first."

Feinberg is a native New Englander, born in Rhode Island and raised in Massachusetts. A graduate of the University of Massachusetts–Amherst, he has worked in Boston radio, and in television throughout the East. "An enthusiastic bird watcher and bad

golfer," he likes birding "because you can take it anywhere. All you need are binoculars and a bird book."

*What did you eat growing up?*

My mom was a great cook. Anything but fish. Her hamburgers were more like meat loaf patties—with garlic, chopped onions, celery, egg, and bread crumbs. Great.

*How'd you learn to cook?*

I was always pretty self-sufficient. I don't cook much from recipes, though. It's more like, what do we got? I don't have many complaints from friends. Like most men—if we can stereotype—I barbecue. Ribs are my favorite. Driving out here, in fact, was the Great Rib Tour. Surprisingly, the best I found were in El Paso at The Rib Hut.

*What's your favorite fast food?*

I'll bring some fruit to work with me, or grab a seven-layer burrito at Taco Bell. If I'm home, I'll sauté up some Bermuda onion, mushrooms, and red peppers and throw them on a Boboli crust with some olives and pepperoni, and bake at 475 degrees for fifteen minutes.

*Your favorite healthful food?*

Fruit, salad with nonfat dressing, or baked tortilla chips with roasted garlic salsa from Trader Joe's.

*Your most hated food?*

Chopped liver. All our relatives would say my mom's was the best. "Take it, enjoy it," they'd say. But my two brothers and I wouldn't eat it.

*What's your favorite sinful food?*

Do I have to pick just one? I love ice cream, and chocolate. Cadbury. Hershey. Nestle's Crunch. Bark-white chocolate with almonds. One summer I made an important discovery: that peanut M&Ms and a good ale like Molson's Golden make for a wonderful combination. I gained ten pounds that summer. Now I don't keep the two around.

*What would your last meal be?*

Some barbecued ribs, if they'd let me make them. Or boiled Maine lobstah with red bliss potato salad and sweet co'n. My tombstone would read, "He lived to eat," or "He loved to eat." They're interchangeable.

## AL'S FRIEND SHARON'S CAESAR-AT-HIS-FINEST SALAD

**DRESSING:**
3 tablespoons olive oil
1 tablespoon vegetable oil
juice of 2 medium-size lemons
4 cloves garlic, mashed
1 inch tubed anchovy paste
6 shakes Tabasco sauce (or to taste)
4 shakes Worcestershire sauce
1 coddled egg* (optional)
⅛ teaspoon dry mustard

**SALAD:**
1 large head romaine lettuce, washed, dried, and ripped into small pieces
4 tablespoons freshly grated Parmesan (or Romano) cheese
1 cup large croutons

*Using a fork, mix all the ingredients for the dressing in a large wooden bowl. Add the romaine and toss. Add the croutons and toss again. Sprinkle with the cheese and serve to "four friends who'll enjoy this garlic-lovers' delight-with-a-bite,"* says Al Feinberg.

**Coddled is not quite soft-boiled. Eileen cooks the egg, in the shell, for 1½ minutes in boiling water.*

# Bill Frieder

BILL AND LAURA FRIEDER, PEELING THEIR FAVORITE.

ASU basketball coach Bill Frieder is that rarity, a coach who didn't play basketball in college. A native of Saginaw, Michigan, he earned his bachelor's and master's degrees in business administration from Michigan University, and spurned several business offers after graduation, opting to coach high-school basketball instead. He was head coach at Michigan from 1981 through 1989, where he compiled a 191–87 record and was named National Coach of the Year.

In the seven years he's coached at ASU, he has had 122 wins in 210 games. Former USC coach George Raveling said of Frieder's impact, "In thirty years, I don't know of a coach who has turned around a program the way Frieder has."

Frieder and his wife, Janice, live in

*Tempe. They have one daughter, Laura, seventeen, who is a state champion—show jumper and a freshman in the honors program at ASU.*

*What did you eat as a child?*

I grew up in the produce business in Saginaw. When I was out in the stock-yards and city markets selling fruits and vegetables, I'd grab a loaf of bread, and get a tomato and some cheese. Or make a little fruit salad with some leftover fruit. My parents were always gone. At home I'd bake a potato and throw a can of corn or beans on it. That's the way I grew up.

In 1965, before I got married, I wanted to lose some weight, so all I ate were salads and oranges for three months. I weighed 150 then. Now I weigh 170, the most I've ever weighed. But I guess that's not too bad.

*What do you eat now?*

I love potatoes. I eat potatoes in some form every day. My daughter Laura loves potatoes, too. One day when she was thirteen or fourteen, we spent the whole afternoon and evening making potatoes every way we could think of: baked, French-fried, twice-baked, mashed, scalloped, and broasted. We had a lot of fun.

*What's the best meal you ever had?*

I have no idea. I don't know what a good meal is. My wife would have to tell you what that was. I'm not that sophisticated. My preference is to go somewhere I can get a soup and sandwich.

*What's your favorite sinful food?*

Oh, the typical junk food—a hamburger and French fries. When I decide to eat properly, I do a pretty good job. But you know what? I could eat cherry pie à la mode or a hot-fudge sundae every day.

*What restaurants do you like?*

We do a lot of our recruiting at Don & Charlie's. Kids love it. And we'll go to Keegan's, Chianti, McDuffey's, Monti's, or Nello's Pizza.

*Are there any foods you hate?*

I don't really like escargot. I don't know what it is, but it doesn't sound good. I once passed up a trip to China because I heard you had to eat octopus and eel. I sent Cotton Fitzsimmons in my place. He called me when he got home and said, "You made the right decision."

## SWEDISH GREEN POTATOES

*"This is best if made up and refrigerated, then baked the next day," says Janis Frieder. "I serve it with grilled tenderloin, fresh asparagus, and a salad. Everyone loves it."*

8 large potatoes, peeled and cut into 1-inch pieces
¾ cup sour cream
1 teaspoon sugar
4 tablespoons butter
2 teaspoons salt
¼ teaspoon pepper
2 tablespoons snipped chives
¼ tablespoon snipped dill
1 (10-ounce) package frozen chopped spinach, cooked and well drained
1 cup shredded cheddar cheese

*In a large pot, boil, drain, and mash potatoes. Add the sour cream, sugar, and butter, and beat until fluffy. Add the remaining ingredients.*

*Preheat oven to 400°F. Place the potatoes in a greased baking dish. Bake 30 minutes or until bubbly.*

*Serves 8.*

# Joe Garagiola

*Joe Garagiola used wit to parlay his position as a third-string catcher with the St. Louis Cardinals into a thirty-year career with NBC-TV. A Phoenix resident since 1977, Garagiola and his wife, Audrie, have three children: Joe Jr., a local attorney; Steve, a Detroit sports commentator; and Gina, a freelance writer who contributes regularly to* Guideposts *magazine.*

*Now on the* Today *show's farm team, Garagiola has no set deal with the network, he says. "I just do an occasional 'Joe story.'"*

*How'd you learn to cook?*

I didn't. All I can do is toast an English muffin. If I'd stayed in New York any longer, I'd have died of malnutrition or frostbite from all those frozen dinners.

*What's your favorite sinful food?*

Ice cream! I'm like Will Rogers; I never met a flavor I didn't like. My favorite is Ben & Jerry's Chunky Monkey.

*What's your favorite healthful food?*

Bread was a big staple when I was growing up. It was nothing for me to sit down and eat eight or nine pieces of bread. Audrie changed my eating habits for the good. Broccoli? Used to be, I not only wouldn't eat it, I couldn't spell it. Now, we have a salad with every meal, and we eat a lot of fruit and vegetables. It's like perpetual Lent at our house. If it weren't for Audrie, I'd be the Good-year Blimp. I'd be flying over the Fiesta Bowl.

*Was your mother a good cook?*

Yes, and my father was a good cook, too. My parents were both immigrants, and we didn't have much money. What I remember is my mother's Carne à Potate on Fridays, when it was a sin to eat meat. I think it had some meat in it but she'd say, "Where's the meat? Look for it!" My father made polenta with rabbit. We used to joke that we thought it was rabbit but the tomcat was missing. I don't know, maybe he [the cat] went to the witness protection program.

*Does Audrie cook rabbit?*

Oh, no. She won't eat it either. You can't kill the Easter Bunny.

*What foods do you hate?*

Sauerkraut and brussels sprouts. Outside of that, I pretty much eat everything.

*What are your favorite fast foods?*

I'm like everybody else. Wendy's, McDonald's, Jack in the Box. My idea of a balanced meal is not dropping it when you walk to the car.

*Do your kids cook?*

Sure. Our Joe likes to barbecue, Gina likes to bake, and Steve makes great banana bread. He cooks; he cleans; he makes guys like me look bad.

*Where do you like to eat out?*

In my old neighborhood in St. Louis, I like Cunetto's, Zia's, Agusti's, Anthony's, and Dominic's. Here, I like Mancuso's, Steamers, Avanti's, Macayo's, Los Olivos. I can't stand sushi. It's like Jackie Mason said, "Would you go to a place where they don't have a stove?"

*What's your all-time peak culinary experience?*

Risotto. My Audrie's is the best.

*What should your tombstone say?*

On one side it would say, "I can't be in heaven if they don't have risotto." On the other, "I knew I was in trouble when they had Alka-Seltzer on draft."

## RISOTTO ALLA MILANESE

*"This is even better cold than hot, or heated up the next day."*

½ cup butter
2 tablespoons cooking oil
3 slices bacon
4 large onions, diced
8 chicken livers, chopped
1 teaspoon salt
½ teaspoon black pepper
5 cups uncooked rice
10½ cups (about 5 14½-ounce cans) chicken broth
½ teaspoon saffron threads
1 cup chopped fresh mushrooms

*Place the butter, oil, and bacon in a large skillet; heat until the bacon starts to brown. Add the onions and cook until medium brown. Add the livers, salt, and pepper, and stir. Brown for about 5 minutes. Add the rice, stir well, and cook for 2 minutes.*

*Place the broth in a 2-quart saucepan and bring to a boil. Add the boiling broth to the rice mixture; stir well and simmer on very low heat, uncovered, for 25 minutes. Add the saffron and mushrooms and stir well.*

*If the rice seems too dry, add a little more chicken broth.*

*Serves 6.*

# Terry Goddard

COOKING WITH MONICA LEE.

Former Phoenix mayor Terry Goddard grew up in Tucson, the son of Sam and Judy Goddard. (His parents moved to Phoenix in 1964, when the senior Goddard was elected governor.) After graduating from Harvard in 1969, Goddard served in the navy and earned his law degree from ASU in 1976.

He served as mayor of Phoenix from 1984 to 1990 and was the Democratic nominee for governor in 1990. Arguably one of Phoenix's leading mayors, his vision has resulted in several historic preservation projects, as well as downtown redevelopment and cultural projects, including the building of a new city library, history museum, art museum, and science museum, and the renovation of the Orpheum Theatre.

Currently he is in private practice. He is the Arizona state coordinator for

HUD, and serves on the National Trust for Historic Preservation.

Goddard's wife, Monica Lee, is a television producer. They live in a 1912 Craftsman bungalow in the Roosevelt district of central Phoenix.

---

*You are known for your love of good food. What'd you eat as a kid?*

Basic meat and potatoes. My mother is a very good cook. And a friend of my parents would come in and make southern-fried chicken and the best sweet rolls I ever tasted. On Sundays, my granddad bought us all dinner after church, usually at the cafeteria at Frampton and Stone. I thought pushing a tray and getting anything I wanted was just wonderful.

*When did you learn to cook?*

I had an early talent for cooking. When I was six or seven, my mother left me the ingredients for a layer cake, which I made, adding green food coloring. I was cooking in the living room and the carpet later had a big green spot that never came out.

*You later wrote restaurant reviews, as I recall.*

Yes, that was in the late seventies. I wrote anonymous reviews for the *Phoenix Business Journal*. Great job; I never could have afforded to eat where they sent me. In fact, I did the first rave review of Vincent's, two months ahead of Craig Claiborne. I always thought I was ahead of *The New York Times*.

*What restaurants do you like now?*

Vincent's continues to be delightful, and I've had great lunches at Christopher's Bistro. We also like Mi Patio, Such Is Life, Tarbell's, Crazy Jim's, and anywhere Norman Fierros happens to be cooking.

*Do you and Monica cook together?*

Yes, we did Easter dinner together for my folks. I grilled the meat and made the rolls and bread. Monica produced the entire meal.

*What should your tombstone say?*

"He ate well, and often." I eat an impressive amount of food, but I'm blessed with a really good metabolism.

---

## TERRY GODDARD'S GRILLED FLANK STEAK

*"This is easy, flavorful, and cheap—all my favorite qualities in food. Serve with wide-sliced veggies, lightly brushed with oil and grilled alongside the steak."*

4 cloves garlic, minced
4 tablespoons red wine (or vinegar)
4 tablespoons lemon juice
3 teaspoons Dijon mustard
1½ teaspoons Worcestershire sauce
1 teaspoon soy sauce
½ teaspoon red pepper flakes
1 (2½-pound) flank steak

*In a medium-size, nonmetal bowl, combine all the ingredients except the steak. Mix well and pour into a large, sealable plastic bag with the steak; refrigerate 6 to 8 hours.*

*Remove steak from the plastic bag, reserving marinade. Grill the steak over hot coals about 5 to 7 minutes on each side, basting with the marinade. Slice very thin against the grain.*

*Serves 3 hungry or 6 regular eaters.*

# $\mathcal{B}$arry Goldwater Jr.

Barry Goldwater Jr. grew up in Phoenix, the son of a community volunteer mother and father who was a merchant before turning politician.

He earned his degree in business from ASU in 1962, planning to enter the family business, Goldwaters department store, "but that was the year they sold the company.

"I had polished the brass and worked in the stockroom all the time I was growing up, expecting to join the store," he said. "But I wasn't going to go to work for some conglomerate."

So he became a stockbroker in Los Angeles and "made a million riding the bull market up in the '50s."

Then, he said, "I kind of got sucked into running for Congress"—and won. "All of a sudden, I was a Congressman."

Barry and his father lived together briefly in Washington. "That didn't *last too long because we'd argue about who was going to take out the garbage,"* he said.

*After thirteen years in Congress, Goldwater moved back to L.A., where he worked as a business consultant. From 1993 to 1995, he helped Geordie Hormel with his business affairs. He is now a financial consultant and lobbyist.*

---

*Was your mother a good cook?*

Not particularly, but she could make good beans, and she made a great salad. We ate regular food—I can't remember what, really—but we did eat at home all the time.

*Do you cook much now?*

Sure, but I'm a bachelor so things gotta be easy for me. I don't get excited about food. Eating's just like water or air—I have to have food. But my philosophy is, if you gotta do it, do it well.

*What do you eat?*

Fruit and vegetables. Lamb, shrimp, or chicken. Lamb's my favorite meat. Actually, I stir-fry or fix pasta almost every night. Sometimes I'll make a sauce. If you can make sauce, you can make any-thing taste good. A good sauce for lamb is 1½ tablespoons vinegar, a pinch of salt, a half teaspoon salt, a pinch of dry mustard, a couple cloves of minced garlic, and a third cup of salad oil. It's great to brush on lamb before grilling.

*Have a favorite sinful food?*

Anything chocolate: cookies, ice cream. I love the desserts chef Brian Cheney makes at the Wrigley Mansion, especially his chocolate fudge cake.

*Your father likes chili. Do you?*

I hate chili. There's nothing nutritious about it, and it talks to you for two days! Anybody who says they love chili, I look at them twice.

*What restaurants do you like?*

Here, I like Baby Kay's, Pischke's, the Wrigley Mansion, and the Blue Burrito. In L.A. I like Morton's, Jerry's Deli, and Maria's.

*What was your peak dining experience?*

I always enjoyed eating at the White House. It wasn't the food. The food was great but it was the aura, being around that much power. I sat with Anwar Sadat and Menachem Begin at the state dinner when they signed the peace accord.

Every time I went to the White House I stole something—an ashtray or a spoon. The biggest thing I ever stole was a chair. Oh, I didn't really steal it; they gave it to me after it broke when I was sitting in it.

## BARRY GOLDWATER JR.'S CHICKEN-IN-A-BAG

1 whole (2- to 3-pound) chicken
1 teaspoon salt
½ teaspoon pepper
½ teaspoon garlic powder
1 teaspoon paprika
2 tablespoons butter

*Preheat oven to 400°F.*

*Wash and thoroughly dry chicken. Put chicken and dry ingredients in a big paper grocery sack. Shake it. Open sack and pat butter over chicken. Seal bag with twist ties. Bake for 1½ hours with a pan underneath to collect drippings.*

*Let oven cool before opening door. "Throw away chicken and eat bag. Just kidding. It's the most tender, crispy chicken you'll ever eat."*

*Serves 6.*

# R. C. Gorman

Courtesy of Navajo Gallery

Artist R. C. Gorman was born on the Navajo Reservation, where he went to a one-room school. After high school, he joined the navy at nineteen and returned to Arizona in 1955 to attend NAU. He later studied in Mexico, and painted in San Francisco during the early 1960s, supplementing his income by posing in the nude for other artists.

In 1968, he moved to Taos, New Mexico, and opened the Navajo Gallery. In 1973, he was the only living Indian painter to be included in the American Indian Art exhibition at New York's Metropolitan Museum of Art. He has printed, painted, and exhibited throughout the U.S., and in France, Spain, and Japan. In 1986, he was honored by Harvard University with the Humanitarian Award in Fine Arts.

He has lived for almost thirty years on a ninety-acre spread north of Taos, in a grand fifteen-room home that started as an eighteenth-century sheep shack. There, he entertains often, with the help of Rose Roybal, his cook and close friend of eighteen years.

Lunch guests have included Arnold Schwarzenegger, Elizabeth Taylor, Cloris Leachman, Danny DeVito, Sandy Duncan, Ruth Warwick, and Congressman Bill Richardson. Jacqueline Onassis also came to see Gorman but she didn't get lunch. "You have to call ahead if you want lunch," he says. "Rose insists." The only person Rose might break her rule for is Al Pacino. "She idolizes him. She met him at the St. Regis in New York, but even before that, she had his pictures up all over the refrigerator."

*What did you eat growing up on the reservation?*

You're going to gross out. We ate mutton ribs; blood sausage; sheep innards, called tripitas; and borrienantes, sheep's head. My grandma used to make goat cheese, too. She'd take a little coffee can out under a tree and make goat cheese out there.

*Did you learn to cook?*

During the Second World War, when I was a kid, my mother was working for the war causes, and my father was in the war [his father, Carl Gorman, was one of the famous Navajo Codetalkers who enciphered U.S. war messages]. I was the oldest kid, so I had to cook for my brothers and sisters. I made fried potatoes and beans. And we always had Spam in those days.

*And now, what do you like?*

Now that I live here, Rose has gotten me addicted to chiles. My favorite is her pork with red chiles. Yesterday she made a green chile stew. We always have company for lunch. Today we had lamb chops and we made the plumber stay. Rose likes him because she thinks he's a hunk.

*What do you like in healthful foods?*

What? I wouldn't look the way I do if I liked health foods.

*You travel a great deal. What's your secret to finding good food while traveling?*

If you want to eat well, find a good cook and take her with you. Rose steals recipes here and there throughout the world.

*You have published cookbooks yourself. Tell us about them.*

I've published three volumes of *Nudes & Foods* [one of them from Northland Publishing].

My gallery director, Virginia Dooley, edits them. She's a gourmet cook, too. She always cooks for me on Sundays. She experiments on me.

*Where do you get the recipes for the books?*

From everyone. You get a free book if you give us a recipe or if you pose in the nude.

*What restaurants do you like?*

In Taos, I like Joseph's Table, The Trading Post, Lambert's, Villa Fontana, Casa Cordova, The Renegade, Jacquelina's, and I take chile fiends to Chile Connection. If a restaurant doesn't have a good wine list, you can count me out.

## ROSE'S RED CHILE

*"Everyone loves this," says Gorman.*

8 pork chops
2 quarts water
2 tablespoons lard
4 tablespoons flour
3 tablespoons Chimayo dry red
   chile powder
1 teaspoon salt
12–16 flour tortillas

*Cook the pork chops in the water in a pressure cooker for 45 minutes. Debone and cube the pork chops, saving the juice.*

*In a large skillet, melt the lard over low heat. Gradually add the flour and chile powder; cook 3 minutes, stirring constantly. Add the juice from the pressure cooker, the pork chops, and the salt. Simmer on very low heat for 40 minutes. Don't let it burn!.*

*Serve in bowls with flour tortillas. Serves 6 to 8.*

# Zarco Guerrero

Artist, musician, and playwright Zarco Guerrero is best known for his hand-carved masks. PBS has broadcast an hour documentary about his art, and in 1986 he was awarded the prestigious Japan Fellowship from the National Endowment for the Arts, and spent a year in Kyoto, Japan, studying with master mask makers.

An Arizona native, he has studied in Bali, Indonesia, China, and Mexico. Five years ago he played the male lead and co-composed the score for La Mascarada, a play by Childsplay, which was featured at the Kennedy Center in Washington, D.C. In 1993, he received the Governor's Arts Award, and last March was awarded the Scottsdale Arts Council Chairman's Artist Award.

*Guerrero and his wife, Carmen, live in Tempe with their children, Quentzal, fifteen; Tizoc, eight; and Zarina, six. Quentzal plays jazz violin and blues guitar with his parents in their well-known Latin/world beat band, Zum Zum Zum.*

---

*Did you learn to cook as a child?*

Yes, my mother was a fantastic cook, famous for her tortillas and tamales. She used to tell me I was never going to find a woman who could cook as good as she did, so I'd better learn. Fortunately, she was wrong.

*What's the first thing you cooked?*

When I left home at eighteen to live in New York, I remember asking, now how do I make those beans again? The secret is a whole onion, plenty of garlic, and comino [ground cumin].

*Is Carmen a good cook?*

Fantastic. She makes great Mexican food, and you know she comes from Brazil, which isn't the same food. One prerequisite in our marriage contract was fresh tortillas. She usually makes two

dozen on Sunday morning, and by that night, they're gone.

*What's your favorite fast food?*

Tacos at Guedo's Taco Shop, or a burro at Los Dos Molinos.

*Ever have any cooking disasters?*

[Laughs.] Once, when I was a vegetarian, I made meatballs for albondigas with tofu instead of ground beef, and they just disintegrated in the broth. Another time I put cans of jalapeños instead of chiles in the albondigas. Nobody could eat it either time.

*What's your favorite sweet?*

Carmen makes a decadent chocolate cake, and an incredible poppy seed cake.

*What was your all-time best meal?*

In Thailand, in 1987, every meal was amazing. Recently, I had a Thai catfish at a four-table family place in Las Vegas that blew me away. I'm not sure I could even find it again.

*What would you have for your last meal?*

A chile relleno, rice and beans, and two of Carmen's tortillas. She uses half whole wheat flour, half white flour, and lard—you have to use lard to get the flavor. They're chewy, never too salty, and they fold real easy.

---

### ZARCO'S NANA'S ALBONDIGAS

1 tablespoon vegetable oil
1 medium-size onion, chopped
8 cups water
¼ cup chopped fresh cilantro, plus some for garnish
10 fresh mint leaves
2 teaspoons fresh oregano
1 tablespoon chopped fresh parsley
½ green bell pepper, diced
½ red bell pepper, diced
1 (6-ounce) can diced green chiles
1 cup uncooked white rice
1 (16-ounce can) whole tomatoes
1 pound lean ground round
1½ teaspoons garlic powder
Salt and pepper to taste
Lemon wedges for garnish

*In a 4-quart pot, heat the oil and lightly sauté half the onion. Add the water, 1 tablespoon of the cilantro, 8 mint leaves, 1 teaspoon of oregano, parsley, bell peppers, green chiles, rice, and tomatoes. Bring to a boil; boil 10 to 15 minutes.*

*Meanwhile, mix the ground round with the remaining onion. Add remaining 1 teaspoon oregano and two mint leaves, garlic powder, 2 tablespoons cilantro, and salt and pepper. Blend well and form into 1-inch balls. Sprinkle with more salt and pepper and add to soup while still boiling. Continue to boil about 30 minutes, or until meatballs are cooked.*

*Serve with lemon wedges and fresh cilantro.*

*Serves 8.*

# Paul Hamilton

Blues musician Paul Hamilton, of Small Paul & Drivin' Wheel (blues band) fame, was born in central Phoenix, at Memorial Hospital, six blocks from where he lives. "I've lived here since I was five," he says.

Hamilton got his start in show business singing at the Elks Club. "When I was thirteen, they'd sneak me in and I'd do my little James Brown, screaming and falling on my knees." A few years later, he toured with Dyke & the Blazers, opening for acts like Sam & Dave, James Brown, Wilson Pickett, Otis Redding, and Aretha Franklin. "It was exhilarating, and a learning experience, working with Aretha and the others. I watched how they presented themselves, and incorporated bits and pieces into my own presentation."

From an emcee at the Apollo Theatre

*in Harlem he picked up a bit he still uses on audiences: "Glad to see your face in the place. We invite you to partake of the dance floor, and let us put a hole in your soul, a dip in your hip, a rocket in your pocket, a cut in your strut, a glide in your stride. We'll rock you till you drop, and make you sweat till you get wet!"*

---

*Was your mom a good cook?*

She sure was. You name it, she could make it. Fried chicken. Tacos, chicken and dumplings. Her job was cooking at the crippled children's hospital. Watching my mom — her name was Nancy Cordelia Hamilton — my sisters Shirley and Jean and I learned how to cook. I remember making bacon and eggs when I was about twelve. Another time I spilled grease and it flamed up; that was kinda hairy.

*What was your favorite food growing up?*

Mexican food! My mom made good tacos, enchiladas, and burros. I never mastered enchiladas, but I can make tacos and burros.

*Where do you like to eat out?*

For breakfast, on Sunday, I like The Eggery or The Good Egg. After I get off work, I'll go to the 5 & Diner for their Hungry Man, or their chicken-fried steak, which is excellent. AJ's Barbecue is good, and I like the chicken-fried steak at Mrs. White's [Golden Rule Cafe], too. It's to die for. Yeah. God.

*What healthful foods do you like?*

I eat a lot of salad, but I really don't eat that healthful. I'm not a low-calorie, cholesterol counter; God knows I need to be, but I eat what I like and that's been working for me for fifty years.

*What's your favorite sinful food?*

Pecan pie, and Baskin Robbins' banana splits. Yeah.

*Remember the best meal you ever had?*

No, I've had so many good ones, but the best steak I ever had was chateaubriand at Nantucket Lobster Trap, and the best pie I ever ate was a Dutch apple from Baker's Square. I'm addicted to them.

*What would your last meal be?*

My very last meal? Steak and lobster. A whole lobster, not just the tail.

*What would your tombstone say?*

"Here lies a healthy, well-fed man. He lived his life to the fullest."

## SMALL PAUL'S TACOS

*"Serve with mango or key lime Kool-Aid. That's the only way to eat tacos, especially if you're a nondrinker like me."*

2½ pounds extra-lean ground beef
1 large onion, finely chopped
2 teaspoons seasoned salt
2 teaspoons black pepper
2 teaspoons garlic powder
1 teaspoon chili powder
3 dozen fresh corn tortillas
2 cups corn oil
3 cups grated longhorn
   cheddar cheese
3 cups shredded lettuce
2 cups fresh chopped tomatoes
1 (16-ounce) jar picante salsa

*In a large frying pan, brown the ground beef and onion over medium heat and add the salt, pepper, garlic powder, and chili powder, stirring to mix thoroughly. Remove from the heat and cover.*

*Fry the tortillas in the corn oil in a medium-size frying pan — doubling them over while frying — the way you like them. "I like mine medium: between soft and crispy." (Fry longer for crispy.)*

*Stuff taco shells with the meat mixture, cheese, lettuce, tomatoes, and salsa.*

*Serves 6 to 10 people, depending on their appetites. "I can eat six myself."*

# *B*ill Heywood

*Phoenix radio announcer Bill Heywood has spent more than thirty-five years entertaining his early-morning fans. Twice named* Billboard *magazine's number-one air personality, he was recently selected as Best Radio Host and Media Person of the Year by Arizona Women in Radio & Television. A Kansas native, he moved to the Valley in 1960, and lives near the Arizona Biltmore with his wife, Susan Heywood, a well-known advertising executive.*

*He and his wife are active volunteers for organizations that offer aid to disadvantaged women and children, and homeless animals. They are co-chairs of the 1997 Scratch 'N Sniff Awards, a benefit for the Arizona Humane Society.*

*Was your mom a good cook?*

Both Mom and Grandma were good cooks. We raised chickens and my family fished, too. We had fourteen tons of fish in the freezer at any time. I hated fish, especially carp, which is mostly bone, with an ounce or two of fish. We had fried chicken all the time, too. My grandmother didn't even use an ax to kill them; she'd wring their necks. They ate every part of the chicken: the feet, the beaks. Now I only eat free-range chickens. That's chickens who are free to jump into the range by themselves.

*Did you cook as a kid?*

No, the only thing I did in the kitchen was lick the pan. "Little Billy gets to lick the pan." But later on, I made myself fried Spam sandwiches on toast. I thought it was ham, misspelled—I didn't know what was in it then.

*Ever have any cooking disasters?*

We had some people over one time, and they raved about this wonderful soup we served, and wanted the recipe. It was from Marie Callender's, so Susan finally told them the recipe was a family secret.

*What's your favorite healthful food?*

Hospital food? I like meat loaf through an IV. Oh, healthful food—I like the tofu scramble at Marche Gourmet. I don't know what tofu is. It sounds healthy but it's probably just fried snot, imported from Formosa.

*Any favorite fast foods?*

Sure, a turkey sandwich at Pugzie's or Duck 'n Decanter, or a bean enchilada at Taco Bell.

*What sinful food do you crave?*

There's a dessert called Grandma's Outrageous Fantasy Pie at this place in Laguna Beach that has fudge and berries and whipped cream. Four people could eat one piece, but I hog it all.

*A rumor has circulated for years that the only thing Susan makes is reservations. True?*

No, she always could cook; we were just in a period where she chose not to. She's a good cook. Her turkey meat loaf is so good that Laguna, our dog, used to like it better than beef. And her Borger Tacos— that's for Borger, Texas, where she's from—are great. It's a taco that's wrapped up in a flour tortilla. Taco Bell is doing something like it now, but she did it first. We're suing.

*Where do you like to eat out?*

Neighborhood places like Eddie's Grill, Bamboo Club, Ajo Al's, Christopher's, Hops, and we've rediscovered Houston's: we like fresh fish, and on Monday nights they often have fresh halibut.

*Any foods you hate?*

I don't have a good relationship with kiwi. It's green; it's furry; it should be the wheel of a play car you win at the fair.

## SUSAN'S RIGHTEOUS TEXAS TURKEY MEAT LOAF

*"Highly recommended for a cold sandwich the next day," says Heywood. "Spread bread with mayo, a little ketchup, add thick slices of meat loaf; eat and then float off to naptime."*

2 egg yolks
1 (6-ounce) can tomato paste
½ cup frozen corn
½ cup frozen peas
½ cup chopped green bell pepper
⅓ cup chopped red onion
Dash each of garlic powder,
    black pepper, and parsley
1 pound extra-lean ground turkey
⅓ cup White-Cheddar Cheese-its
    (or potato chips)
½ cup ketchup

*Preheat oven to 350°F.*
    *In a large bowl, beat the yolks with the tomato paste. Mix in all the remaining ingredients except the ketchup, adding the turkey and then the chips last. Mold into a glass baking dish and spread the ketchup on top, covering completely. Bake for 1 hour.*
    *Serves 6.*

# ara Hitchcock

Tara Hitchcock, host of KTVK's Good Morning Arizona, was born in Pennsylvania, and grew up in New Jersey and north Dallas, the oldest of four daughters. She earned her bachelor's degree in 1991 from Boston College, and her master's degree from Medill School of Journalism at Northwestern University.

She joined Channel 3 in 1996 after a stint as news anchor at KBMT-TV in Beaumont, Texas.

Hitchcock is single and lives near The Pointe at South Mountain. She enjoys movies, dining out, and traveling. She loves sports, especially Suns games, and hockey and football games. "Oh, man, I cried when ASU lost the Rose Bowl. It becomes this personal thing when you know some of the players."

*What did you grow up eating?*

We used to joke with Mom about her pea omelets. These things were nasty. We'd make fun of her and get grounded until my dad came home. But she and my grandmother made good pirogi and kielbasa. My dad cooked, too. In fact, he won the neighborhood chili cook-off five years in a row.

*What'd you first cook?*

I made an omelet for my dad's breakfast, but since I couldn't do the whole flipping-and-folding thing, I really just put cheese on scrambled eggs.

*Ever have any cooking disasters?*

Several. I remember cooking for boyfriends. You know, the dinner you get so excited about. One time, my boyfriend and I got sidetracked really bad watching a movie, and I burned the chicken. We ordered out. Chinese.

*What's in your fridge right now?*

Orange juice, milk, and yogurt that's probably rotted.

*What do you eat now?*

A lot of the foods I hated growing up. I used to hate spinach until I had the spinach-and-artichoke dip at Houston's. I still hate liver, string beans, and pea omelets.

*Do you crave any sinful foods?*

Bacon cheeseburgers, Snickers Bars, ice cream, and peanut butter. I used to put peanut butter on everything, and I've had to work really hard to cut out ice cream. But I eat constantly on the show.

*What's your peak dining experience?*

It would have to be the dinner a friend and I had at the Different Pointe of View. Chef Beeson gave us the best seat in the house, and we had everything. Sea bass. Lamb. Duck. Shrimp. He even made us Bananas Foster, himself. I thought, man, this is going to cost us a fortune, but I didn't care. I didn't eat for like a week after that.

*What other restaurants do you like?*

One of the things I like best about Phoenix is all the great restaurants we have. I like Tarbell's, Sam's Cafe, Christopher's, and Sandale at the Hyatt Gainey Ranch. And Dan Davis has gotten me hooked on The Monastery.

### BABCI'S LOBSTER THERMIDOR

*"This was my grandmother Babci's recipe. She had a big influence on our lives, and she taught me to make this. It's excellent."*

1 2-pound lobster
1 teaspoon peppercorns
¼ cup chopped celery
½ cup chopped mushrooms
2 tablespoons butter
½ pint heavy cream
1 teaspoon dry mustard
1 tablespoon cooking sherry
¼ cup Parmesan cheese

*Boil the lobster with the peppercorns and celery just until lobster is opaque; drain, reserving peppercorns and celery. Remove shell from the lobster and cut into 1-inch chunks. Set aside.*

*Preheat oven to 350°F.*

*Sauté the mushrooms in the butter. In a large casserole dish, mix the reserved peppercorns and celery, mushrooms, cream, mustard, and sherry. Add lobster chunks. Top with the cheese and bake 20 minutes.*

*Serves 2.*

# eordie Hormel

GEORDIE AND JAMIE HORMEL WATCH GERI AND GILLIAN BAKE COOKIES.

George A. Hormel II grew up in Austin, Minnesota, where his grandfather, for whom he was named, founded the Hormel Company in 1891.

He worked with Hormel as president of Dinty Moore Products, but left the company in 1955. After a move to California, Hormel founded The Village Recorder in 1968, a recording studio that recorded hits by such groups as Fleetwood Mac, Steely Dan, and Frank Zappa. Hormel lives in the McCune (now Hormel) Mansion with his wife, Jamie, and their daughters, Geri and Gillian George. He owns and operates the historic Wrigley Mansion, "which was built in 1929, one year after I was."

*Do you cook?*

Not anymore. But I have. I used to make two famous things: Dinty Moore Beef Stew and Mary Kitchen Roast Beef Hash. At one time, I made Hormel's Onion Soup. I loved to take people in there: The room was a Green Giant factory the size of a high-school gymnasium, full of women peeling onions. It was like walking into a roomful of tear gas. Visitors never realized that in two to three minutes you became immune to it.

*What's your favorite healthful food?*

Beans. All kinds. But I don't cook meat. We haven't had any meat for awhile. I'm not a strict vegetarian but I've been against eating meat since about 1960. A little animal fat's okay only if you're an Eskimo.

*What's your favorite fast food?*

Take some plain yogurt—and I'm partial to any brand not affected by bovine hormones—and add a little real maple syrup. It's better than any flavored yogurt.

*What's your most hated food?*

Hydrogenated oil. Our bodies can't break it down. The only acceptable oil is expeller-pressed extra-virgin olive oil. Everyone should start reading labels and stop using this stuff—it's worse than Spam!

*I take it you don't eat Spam.*

It's not on my diet. But Spam is the number-one processed meat in the world—by far. You'll find it in the finest restaurants in Hawaii, and they even have Spam luaus. I couldn't believe it myself. Lots of people are very serious about their Spam.

*What was your peak culinary experience?*

Butternut Squash Soup, last night at the Wrigley Mansion. I always think of the most recent meal I've had. Here in town, I like Christopher's, The Phoenician, Scottsdale Princess, The Wigwam, and the Wrigley. I eat most often at the Wrigley. I feel we've reached a point where every meal there is the best. We've had five years to get to this point. We're moving from fine European cuisine to health-oriented organic cuisine. If we weren't serving the best food, I'd close it up now. I'm losing too much money to serve bad food.

*What would be your last meal?*

I wouldn't have one. I'd spend the time with my lawyer.

## WRIGLEY MANSION'S BUTTERNUT SQUASH SOUP

½ cup chopped onion
2 tablespoons butter
2 medium butternut squash, skin removed, and coarsely chopped into (2 cups) ½-inch squares
¼ teaspoon thyme
¼ teaspoon oregano
¾ cup chicken stock
¼ teaspoon salt
Pinch of white pepper
½ cup heavy cream
¼ cup crème fraîche for garnish
Pinch of freshly grated nutmeg for garnish

*Heat a heavy saucepan on medium-high for 2 to 3 minutes. Sauté the onions in 1 tablespoon of the butter until the onions are caramelized. Add the squash, thyme, and oregano, continuing to sauté until the squash is soft. Add the chicken stock and simmer, uncovered, for 15 minutes. Purée the mixture in a blender or food processor, and add the salt, pepper, and remaining 1 tablespoon of butter; continue to blend. In a small saucepan, reduce cream by one-half over medium heat and add to soup. Blend again.*

*Garnish with crème fraîche and nutmeg and serve hot.*

*Serves 4.*

*For less fat, add ¼ cup more chicken stock and substitute canola or olive oil for the butter. Use whipped nonfat milk for the heavy cream and puréed nonfat cottage cheese for the crème fraîche.*

# Jane Dee Hull

Arizona secretary of state Jane Dee Hull began her career in public service in 1979 when she was elected to represent District 18 in the Arizona House of Representatives.

Elected speaker of the house in 1989, she was the first woman to hold that position. Hull received her bachelor's degree from the University of Kansas, and has done post-graduate work in political science and economics at ASU, where she also serves on ASU's Dean's Council of 100.

She and her husband, Dr. Terrance Hull, live in north Phoenix. They have four children and eight grandchildren.

As secretary of state, Hull is next in line to become governor.

*What did you grow up eating?*

Basics like pot roast, meat loaf, and lots of potatoes. We grew up eating for the Chinese, like everyone of that time. "Eat, eat. Think of the starving children in China."

My father was a newspaperman and my mother stayed at home with us. I remember my father covering that big plane crash over the Grand Canyon in 1956. He filed from the bar at El Tovar, and scooped everyone.

*What did you first cook?*

When Terry and I first got married, I remember making something called a Lazy Daisy Cake. That was all I had ever cooked. Terry taught me how to boil water for eggs. Even now, after forty-three years of marriage, my philosophy is, if you can't cook it in one pan, I don't cook it. What kept the marriage together all these years was, I always told Terry, "If we split, you get the kids."

*Ever have any cooking disasters?*

The funniest thing was one time when I was making flan for a bridge luncheon. I melted the sugar in a Pyrex pan right on the stove and it blew up. I had glass from here to high water all over my kitchen.

*What do you cook now?*

If we eat at home, it's usually meat, vegetables, or salad. Also, I have a dozen Lean Cuisines in the freezer at any given time, which is a very comfortable feeling.

*Have any favorite sinful foods?*

Yes. The JD pie at Rock Springs. It's a pecan pie made with Jack Daniels, and it's the best thing I've ever tasted. Also, the tiramisù at Salute's. I go in spurts. For a while, it was M&Ms with peanuts, then it was candied orange slices. And popcorn: I could live on popcorn.

*What restaurants do you like?*

Salute's, Christo's, Mandarin Delight, and El Bravo. And I love Vincent's, especially his crème brûlée and duck tamales, which are marvelous.

## SHRIMP SAUSAGE HORS D'OEUVRES

*"Serve with a loaf of French bread, sliced or torn into pieces."*

½ cup andouille sausage, chopped
2 tablespoons olive oil
¼ cup chopped shallots
6 ounces uncooked shrimp, peeled
½ cup roasted red peppers, diced*
2 tablespoons chopped fresh parsley (or 3 teaspoons dried)
1 tablespoon chopped fresh thyme (or 1 teaspoon dried)
1 tablespoon Dijon mustard

*In a medium-size pan, brown the sausage in the oil; transfer to a bowl. Place the shallots and the shrimp in the pan and cook, stirring, for 2 minutes. Mix in the remaining ingredients, stirring until hot.*
*Serves 6.*

*\*Roast red peppers by cutting into wide strips and placing under the broiler, skin side to the flame. Allow skin to blacken; peel and discard skin.*

# Waylon Jennings

*Country superstar Waylon Jennings grew up in west Texas and got his start at age nineteen playing bass for Buddy Holly. He lived in Phoenix in the early 1960s; while headlining at JD's in Tempe he recorded his first hit, "Stop the World and Let Me Off," in Nashville.*

*He is the first country artist to sell a million copies of one album, and the first artist to have a five-million seller. Jennings recently recorded a duet with Neil Diamond for Diamond's newest album, and joined his 1995 tour of Australia, Japan, Hawaii, and Hong Kong.*

*He lives near Nashville with Jessi Colter, his wife of twenty-six years, and their seventeen-year-old son, Shooter. His 1996 autobiography, Waylon (Time-Warner), has sold more than 100,000 copies and received critical acclaim.*

*What did you eat growing up?*

I was what they called a beans and 'taters boy. I came after the Depression but we still felt it. My dad worked sunup to sundown for a dollar a day, and sometimes we flat didn't have any food. Once when I was two and a half, we walked down to this man's house and he gave us something to eat. I remember it was the first time I saw a refrigerator and linoleum. At home we had a dirt floor. Another winter when my dad didn't have a job, we ate beans and corn bread every meal.

Growing up, we ate things we invented, like crackers in chocolate milk, or biscuits with butter, sugar, and coffee over them.

*What do you like to eat now?*

Jessi's taught me more about food than I ever knew. I've gone 180 degrees from the foods I grew up on. I'm a diabetic and I'm on a low-fat diet, but I eat better food than most anybody I know. It's not like prison or anything. I'll have Egg-beaters and an English muffin for breakfast, homemade vegetable soup or a tuna or cheese sandwich for lunch, and a regular dinner. The trick is to stay out of the cupboard in between.

In a restaurant, I tell them I'll fall on the floor and have a fit if they bring me what I can't have. They basically say yes to everything.

*What's your favorite sinful food?*

Chocolate anything. Or sausage gravy and biscuits with cheese eggs. My favorite meal is breakfast, and nobody can fix it like Jessi. In one week I could gain twenty pounds.

*What was it like touring with Buddy Holly?*

All I had ever known was beans and bread. They had me treed in New York.

The waitress was so rude at this deli we went to that she scared me half to death. I ordered a sandwich, I think it was pastrami, and I'd never tasted anything like that. After one bite, I put it in my pocket so she wouldn't yell at me.

*What do you cook?*

I can't boil water but I can make Eggs-in-a-Raft. You cut a hole in toast and fry an egg in it. One time I burned them but Shooter said, "Dad, these are really good."

*Any foods you hate?*

Anchovies I despise, and anything uncooked—like sushi. Anything that still has a chance to bite me.

*What do you eat on the road?*

We always eat in the best restaurants, but it's hard to know what to order. When we were in Austria, none of us knew that Wiener schnitzel was veal cutlet until the day after we left. We never could make them understand iceberg lettuce in Australia. Our friend Edith Kunz said we should cut pictures out of magazines so we could point to them.

*Where do you like to eat in Phoenix?*

Ruth's Chris, Steamers, the Pointe Hilton, and any Bobby McGee's, as long as Bob [Sikora, the owner] isn't cooking.

*What should your tombstone say?*

"Pass the biscuits."

## WAYLON'S LOW-FAT CORN BREAD

1 cup self-rising white cornmeal
1 cup low-fat or fat-free sour cream
2 eggs, or 1 ounce Eggbeaters
2 tablespoons canola oil
Liquid from 1 (15¼-ounce) can cream-style corn, corn discarded

*Preheat the oven to 425°F.*

*Spray a generous amount of Pam on a 9-inch-square glass dish or an iron skillet.*

*In a medium-size bowl, mix all the ingredients. Pour the batter into the baking pan. Bake for 35 minutes.*

*Serves 4.*

# Bil Keane

*Bil Keane began syndicating his Family Circus cartoons in 1960 in nineteen newspapers. Today, the family-based panel is seen in 1,500 newspapers worldwide, including* The Arizona Republic. *He has published sixty-five books and received several awards including the coveted Reuben from the National Cartoonists Society, "Our version of the Oscar or Emmy," he notes.*

*Keane and his wife, Thelma, live in a sprawling home in Paradise Valley, where he divides his time between drawing, playing tennis, and entertaining visiting family. The Keanes' children are Gayle, Neal, Glen, Christopher, and Jeff Keane (the latter is Bil's assistant). They have eight grandchildren.*

9-7
© 1996 Bil Keane, Inc.
Dist. by Cowles Synd., Inc.

"Want a good recipe for soup?
Just let your ice cream melt."

*What did you eat as a child?*

My mother was a Philadelphian and she believed in healthy foods. She wasn't fond of hoagies or scrapple; she followed [the advice of] Victor H. Linlahr, who advocated salads. As a teenager, I used to hang out with friends, eating hamburgers and milkshakes.

*Did you cook when you were little?*

Once, when my brother was nine and I was about six, we camped out at a woods near our home. We got a campfire going and decided to cook something, so we cooked some pork and beans. We just put the can in the fire and it kept swelling up. Finally it exploded. We had pork and beans all over the woods and all over us. We didn't eat well that night.

*What are your favorite foods now?*

I love Thel's cooking. She's an excellent cook. Being Australian, she does a fabulous meat pie, which is the equivalent of the hot dog over there. They have meat pie stands at sports events. Thel always cooks when the family comes home—

breaded veal cutlet, stuffed pork chops— and the last few years the daughters-in-law have been trying new things, which are delicious.

*Any favorite sinful foods?*

We don't eat a lot of red meat, but once in awhile I love a great steak and a salad with Roquefort dressing. One of my favorite salads is El Chorro's, with their vinaigrette and crumbled bleu cheese.

*Where else do you like to eat out?*

We enjoy P. F. Chang's, RoxSand's, Frankie's, Shells at Mountain Shadows, Z Téjas, and Drinkwater's, which has a nice view from the veranda. We like tasty foods put together in interesting ways.

*Any foods you can't stand?*

I don't particularly like fish, liver, or kidneys.

*What should your tombstone say?*

"At last—no more health foods."

## THEL'S QUEENSLAND CORN CHOWDER

1 tablespoon butter
1 slice bacon, chopped
1 large onion, finely chopped
3 medium potatoes, peeled and diced
2 carrots, peeled and sliced
1 (16-ounce) can corn, undrained
1 cup water
1 (10-ounce) can cream-of-chicken soup, undiluted
1 soup can milk

*In a medium-size saucepan, sauté the bacon, onion, potatoes, and carrots in the butter for 5 minutes. Add the undrained corn and water. Bring to a boil and simmer, covered, for 10 minutes. Stir in the chicken soup and milk, and heat through but do not boil.*
*Serves 4.*

# on Kyl

U.S. Senator Jon Kyl (R-AZ) grew up in Nebraska and Iowa, "eating good old farm food." He received his undergraduate and law degrees from the University of Arizona, and for the past thirty years has lived in the Phoenix area. He was an attorney with a local law firm for many years, specializing in water issues. In 1986, Kyl was elected to represent Arizona in the U.S. House of Representatives. He served in the House for eight years before earning a seat in the Senate in 1994.

When not in Washington, Kyl lives in the Arcadia/Camelback Mountain area with his wife, Caryll. The Kyls have two grown children, John and Kristi.

*What did you eat as a child?*

We had a little farm outside of town, so we always had beef and plenty of vegetables to eat. Mom was a good cook. Typically we'd have roast beef, mashed potatoes, and four or five kinds of vegetables.

*What do you eat now?*

Whatever I can quickly consume to quench the fire. A ham-and-cheese sandwich, or peanut butter and jelly. I love eating my wife's gourmet food, but I honestly don't care about food that much.

*Did you ever have any cooking disasters?*

Oh, yes. One time I was camping with some guys. We were enjoying cocktail hour overlooking a beautiful valley while I was cooking this great rib-eye steak on a portable hibachi. One of the fellows was careless and managed to kick that rib-eye into the sand. After I killed him, we descended on this one poor guy who had brought chicken take-out with him. He had to share.

*Have any sinful downfalls?*

Oh, sure. I try to stay away from Vincent's crème brûlée. I could live on his duck tamales and crème brûlée.

*Besides Vincent's, what restaurants do you like?*

We enjoy Z Téjas, especially their pork enchiladas. Any place of Paul Fleming's is good. And so is Morton's. We don't go out much as Caryll is a great cook. She and two other women used to do some catering, and they even put out a couple of cookbooks. From Greek to French to Italian. The group still gets together at least once a year. They call themselves "The Kitchen Cabinet."

*What should your tombstone say?*

"He lived to 104. Thankfully, crème brûlée was good for him."

## SOUTHWESTERN PORK ROAST

1 teaspoon chili powder
½ teaspoon salt
½ teaspoon garlic salt
3 pounds boneless pork loin
½ cup ketchup
½ cup apple jelly
1 tablespoon vinegar

*Preheat the oven to 325°F.*

*Mix half of the chili powder with the salt and garlic salt; rub into roast. Cook for 2 to 2½ hours.*

*Ten to 15 minutes before the roast is done, brush the meat with the drippings. When roast is done, drain the pan drippings, measure, and add water to make 1 cup of glaze. Set aside to serve with the roast.*

*Combine ketchup, jelly, vinegar, and the other half teaspoon of the chili powder; pour over the pork and simmer 5 minutes.*

*Serves 6 to 8.*

# G. Gordon Liddy

Syndicated radio talk-show host G. Gordon Liddy is heard in 250 cities throughout the country, and jokes that most of his audience "first learned about me for my role in Watergate, as part of their grade-school homework."

An attorney, Liddy became an FBI agent and at age twenty-nine was the youngest bureau supervisor at FBI national headquarters during the Kennedy administration. He resigned from the FBI to practice international law, and in 1969, ran Richard Nixon's presidential campaign for New York's 28th district.

Under Nixon, Liddy authored the memo that led to the creation of the Drug Enforcement Administration. He resigned his White House post to work on Nixon's second campaign.

Liddy rose to national fame in 1973 for steadfastly refusing to implicate others in the Watergate break-in. Sentenced to more than twenty years in prison, he served five years before he was pardoned by President Jimmy Carter.

He said that his greatest feat is "defeating the best efforts of all three branches of government to force me to become a rat like John Dean." When released from prison, he quoted Nietzsche: "What does not destroy me makes me stronger."

Liddy and his wife have lived in Arizona since 1984. "I kept coming out here to make speeches and found that a number of my very good friends from the FBI had retired here. So we had a built-in circle of friends and wonderful weather. In the summer, you just keep cool in the pool."

*What did you eat when you were a child?*

Peanut-butter-and-jelly sandwiches. My mother made a lot of them.

*What food do you like now?*

I've always eaten healthy food. I consume a considerable amount of deep-ocean, cold-water fish, and vegetables. Fortunately I like both. My daily routine is dry toast with jam, fruit juice, and a cup of decaf for breakfast, two more pieces of dry toast for lunch, and during the four hours I'm broadcasting I eat carrots, celery, and broccoli. For dinner I have fish and more vegetables.

*What about sinful food? Ever have any midnight cravings?*

All my midnight cravings are for sex.

*Do you cook?*

I cook only one thing, and only when I have all the children and grandchildren home. It's a chili recipe that I lack the wit to be able to break down into smaller portions. I came by it when I was in the bowels of one prison where a fellow there, Doc, was famed for his chili, the recipe for which was a deep dark secret.

*What local restaurants do you like?*

Every Sunday we go to Camelback Inn for brunch. During the week we go to Le Peep's for breakfast because Jack, the owner, is a very nice fellow and the food is excellent. If Mrs. Liddy has to go to the bank, we'll go to The Good Egg. In the evenings we go to El Chorro, The Quilted Bear, a new French restaurant in Hilton Village, or a Japanese place near Paradise Valley Mall.

*Does your wife cook?*

After raising five children, she would just as soon not. I consider that Mrs. Liddy has earned anything she wants. She can do and have anything she wants.

*What was your peak dining experience?*

The first meal after I got out of prison. I don't know what I had but it was the best meal of my life. After being in nine different maximum security prisons for five years, I was very happy to be out. Prisons, you see, are populated by two main groups of people. The prisoners themselves who—whatever they may lack in intelligence, cunning, street-smart criminals—are not shy and retiring people. The other half of the population are the guards, people who put themselves in prison for twenty to thirty years. You ask yourself, who would do that? The answer is, very stupid people.

*What should your tombstone say?*

Simply, "G. Gordon Liddy." Because my father told me, "Son, when you gotta tell them who you are, you aren't."

## CHICANO CONVICT GUACAMOLE

*"This I learned from the Chicanos in prison. These ingredients were used because they were what could be smuggled out of the mess hall."*

6 sufficiently ripe avocados, peeled and pitted
4 hard-boiled eggs, peeled and chopped
¾ cup salsa

*Mash the avocados in a large bowl. Mix in the eggs and the salsa. Serve with chips or raw vegetables.*
*As an appetizer this serves 4.*

# Clara Lovett

Dr. Clara Lovett, president of Northern Arizona University, grew up in Trieste, Italy, a port city on the Adriatic Sea. She received her undergraduate degree from the University of Trieste and moved to the United States in 1962, earning a master's and doctoral degree from the University of Texas, Austin.

She taught history at Baruch College and City University of New York during the 1970s, and from 1982 to 1994 lived in Washington, D.C., where she was dean of George Washington University, provost/vice president of George Mason University, and chief of the European division of the Library of Congress. In 1989, she was named one of the one hundred most powerful women in Washington, and in 1992 was honored as Educator of the Year.

Lovett moved to Flagstaff in 1994 with her husband, Dr. Benjamin Brown, a former history professor at the University of Kansas, and retired senior intelligence officer with the CIA.

*What did you eat as a child?*

A lot of fish and vegetables. Not much pasta. My father's side of the family is German and Austrian, and rich pastries were part of the history of my town, so my mother would serve them on Sundays, in rather small quantities.

I grew up in a high-rise apartment in the city, and in the summer we went to the Alps. My brother, Paolo, and I would spend the whole summer in the mountains with our mother; our father would come up on the weekends. He was an actuary for a large insurance company.

*Was your mother a good cook?*

Very good. She's one of those people who never used a recipe except for cakes. She always cooked by feel, taste, and touch.

*When did you learn to cook?*

I was never asked to cook by my mother, and we had help so I didn't cook anything until after I was married. However, I must have absorbed something as I have acquired a sense of seasoning and proportion over the years; we haven't gone hungry, at any rate.

*Ever have any cooking disasters?*

Some notable failures include a pizza crust two inches thick that stuck to the bottom of the pan, and desserts I have thrown out. I will not serve something to guests that I have not tried before.

*Moving to Texas from Italy must have been culture shock. What did you think of the food?*

I lived in a boardinghouse for students, and what I remember most vividly was the quantity and richness of the food. Unbelievable. Many things I liked right away . . . corn bread, barbecue, venison, and Tex-Mex food. Once I learned not to bite hard into jalapeños, I enjoyed the food.

*What are your favorite foods?*

Almost any ripe fruit. Field greens salads. Fish and roast chicken. I have never eaten fried stuff, and I avoid nearly everything that passes for Italian food in this country. Most of it is so heavy you could sink a submarine with it.

*Does your husband cook?*

Yes, but not every often. He is especially good with desserts: things with lots of butter, eggs, and sugar. He has all these killer recipes for things like Texas pecan pie and chocolate-cheese pie.

*What was your most memorable meal?*

I'm fortunate to have eaten in some very famous restaurants and at formal dinners, but what you remember is not so much the food. At the White House, the actual breakfast was not memorable.

*What's your food philosophy?*

I'll try anything once, even Jell-O. You can't avoid Jell-O in Texas.

## RABBIT CACCIATORE

*"Serve over rice, mashed potatoes, or polenta. You can make perfectly good polenta from the cornmeal you get at the store."*

1 (2½-pound) rabbit
1 slice bacon, chopped (optional)
2 tablespoons butter or margarine
1 cup chicken broth
2 medium carrots, finely chopped
2 ribs celery, finely chopped
⅛ teaspoon thyme
1 ripe tomato (or 2 tablespoons tomato sauce)
salt and pepper to taste

*In a large pan, brown the meaty pieces of rabbit and the bacon in the butter or margarine. Add the remaining ingredients and simmer gently, uncovered, for 30 minutes.*
*Serves 2.*

# Harvey Mackay

Author/speaker Harvey Mackay has sold seven million books since publishing his first one, Swim With the Sharks Without Being Eaten Alive (William Morrow). His fourth book, Dig Your Well Before You're Thirsty: The Only Networking Book You'll Ever Need (HarperCollins), was a major Book-of-the-Month club selection, and was a best-seller before it debuted in April. The New York Times named two of Mackay's books to their list of the fifteen best motivational books ever written.

Owner of Mackay Envelope in Minneapolis, Mackay and his wife, Carol Ann, live part of each year in Paradise Valley: "I wrote all my books at the pool at John Gardiner's [now named Gardiner's Tennis Ranch]," he says.

They recently bought a Mummy Mountain lot on which they'll build a new home. "I get turned on by a view," says Mackay.

*What did you grow up eating?*

The truth is dullsville: peanut butter. I can remember eating it in kindergarten. We'd bring our little blankets and eat peanut butter and graham crackers. I just loved it. Still do, fifty-nine years later. I had it yesterday. Gotta be Skippy's Chunky.

*You travel a great deal. What do you eat then?*

I travel 100–150 days a year. I'm always in airports where I've become a TCBY yogurt freak. Carol Ann and I have been to more than seventy countries. She'll eat food from street vendors in Pakistan, Bombay, Karachi, wherever. . . . I eat peanut butter and crackers. I take them with me. But you know what's safe in every country in the world? Ice cream. And the local bread.

*Any foods you hate?*

I won't eat anything that has a strong odor or doesn't look good. Like snails.

*Do you have any sinful foods?*

My downfall is hamburgers. I used to pop for ten to twelve White Castle burgers at a time. But I've conquered that problem since I got into serious running in 1987. I'm a marathoner, and you can't fool around when you're in training. But I'll tell you, I never saw a Snickers Bar I wouldn't unwrap.

*What are your favorite restaurants in Phoenix?*

Head and shoulders above any other place is Vincent's. I have never been served a less-than-spectacular dinner there. We also like Rancho Pinot Grill, and the Arizona Grill. But we eat at home a lot of the time. My wife has a black belt in cooking. She is extraordinarily talented.

*Ever have a peak dining experience?*

Many of them. But one meal will always stand out in my mind. My wife and I had dinner at this restaurant outside Tokyo with *60 Minutes* producer Don Hewitt and his wife. The dollar was godawful then. Prices hit the stratosphere, and our meal came to $1,200 for the four of us. As it turned out, they didn't take credit cards, and we didn't have enough cash on us. We were humiliated. Finally, I negotiated with the owner that she could send someone back to our hotel to pick up the cash. We get into the taxi, laughing our guts out, saying we hoped she understood my shaky Japanese. When we get to the hotel, the owner is standing there in her kimono, waiting for us, with the check in her hand!

## CHILI FOR 200

48 pounds lean, coarsely
   ground beef
48 large onions, chopped
75 cloves garlic, minced
5 cups chili powder
⅓ cup flour
28 (16-ounce) cans whole peeled
   tomatoes
1½ cups salt
6 tablespoons black pepper
1 cup oregano
1 cup white wine vinegar
1 cup brown sugar
2½ cups expensive cognac
15 (27-ounce) cans kidney beans or
   16 (23-ounce) cans pinto beans
   (or combination of both)
20 Spanish onions, chopped
20 cups grated cheddar cheese
20 cups chopped chives

*Brown the ground beef with the large onions and the garlic, divided, in two 48-quart pots. Add the chili powder, flour, tomatoes, salt, pepper, oregano, vinegar, and brown sugar, in halves, to the two pots. Cover and simmer on low, stirring frequently, for 2 hours; add the cognac the last 10 minutes.*

*Meanwhile, in a 40-quart pot, heat the beans, stirring frequently. Add the beans to the chili. Serve with bowls of chopped Spanish onion, grated cheddar cheese, and chopped chives.*

*Serves 200 chili lovers.*

# Merrill Mahaffey

Artist Merrill Mahaffey was raised in Grand Junction, Colorado, where his father was in range management for the U.S. Forest Service. After receiving his MFA degree from ASU, he taught drawing and painting at Phoenix College for thirteen years, leaving education to paint full time in 1980.

Mahaffey's collectors include the Metropolitan Museum of Art, the U.S. Supreme Court, and the Smithsonian Institution. A survey of his work will appear at the Mesa Southwest Museum, and a one-person exhibition at Palm Springs Desert Art Museum. He is represented by Suzanne Brown Gallery of Scottsdale.

He now lives in Santa Fe with his wife, Jeanne, also an artist, spending part of each year in Scottsdale. He has returned to education to teach "How to Be a Professional Artist" at ASU.

*What did you eat as a kid?*

Lots of garden vegetables and deer meat. I didn't know hamburger wasn't made of venison until about the fifth grade. My father was the son of a rancher, and I grew up thinking part of your job as a man was killing enough game that you didn't have to buy meat. Besides deer, we ate rabbit, elk, and mutton, and in the summer we ate fish.

The one thing my father brought home that I wasn't fond of were prairie dogs. One time we even had our own bees. I tried to be macho but I was terrified of them. My ploy was to stand still and hope they didn't see me.

*What did you first cook?*

Eggs. I stole three eggs from the neighbors' chicken coop at the urging of another neighbor boy. I'd never have thought of it. We got a skillet and some butter from my house and built a fire out in the alley, then we cooked them and ate them out of the pan. My diet hasn't changed a whole lot since, but I don't steal eggs anymore.

*Ever have any cooking disasters?*

I made corn bread once that nobody would eat. I had made a small mistake. Instead of one tablespoon of sugar, I put in one cup of sugar.

*What's your favorite sinful food?*

Any kind of fruit pie.

*Is there any food you hate?*

Calf brains . . . most things that other people say are real delicacies, like caviar. And I don't like anything made out of sheep, except wool.

*What's your favorite thing that Jeanne makes?*

She made a tuna casserole, after which I proposed to her in 1976. But her real specialty is corned beef and cabbage, which she always makes on St. Patrick's Day. One time, she opened the pressure cooker and corned beef went everywhere, including the ceiling. What was left in the pot we ate for dinner.

*What should your tombstone say?*

"He wasn't very particular. That's maybe what killed him."

---

## COLORADO RIVER DINNER

1 boat
1 Day-Glo attractor lure with
  barbless hook
3 Snickers Bars
¼ cup cornmeal
1 clove garlic
½ cup extra-virgin olive oil
salt and pepper to taste

*Quietly put boat in the river at Lees Ferry, oaring occasionally. At mile 11.3, cast a lure into the current. Retrieve the attractor alluringly, bringing a huge trout to the beach. Remove the hook carefully. Release the trout immediately and eat the candy.*

# Robert McCall

**LOUISE AND ROBERT McCALL**

*Robert McCall is known worldwide for his paintings of the U.S. space program. Called by Isaac Asimov the nearest thing to an artist-in-residence on outer space, he has documented NASA's space flights since the 1960s. Millions have seen his work at the National Air and Space Museum, and in such movies as* Star Trek *and* 2001: A Space Odyssey. *Several postage stamps have borne his designs, including a 1971 stamp that was canceled on the moon before a global TV audience.*

*McCall lives in Paradise Valley with his wife, Louise McCall, who is herself an artist, painting mostly colorful still lifes.*

*What did you eat as a child?*

I grew up in Columbus, Ohio, and would spend summers on a farm owned by my uncle. I remember so well the wonderful fresh vegetables and fruit. We ate well at home, too. My mother made delicious spareribs and sauerkraut, and strawberry shortcake. One thing I miss terribly here is a good tomato. When I order sliced tomatoes in even the finest of restaurants, I can count on their being tasteless.

*What do you eat now?*

We love Italian food. Marinara sauce on angel hair pasta. Beautiful salads. And Greek food. The feta cheese is what makes it so delicious. I'm not that knowledgeable about wines, but I like merlot. I don't think I've been influenced by the fact that it seems to be a hot wine now.

*Do you cook much?*

No, I never have. Louise has always tried to interest me, but she fixes the meal and I wash the dishes. It's not a bad deal at all. Louise makes wonderful stews. She's a master.

*Any foods you hate?*

Raw oysters. To me, they are slippery, yucky, and obnoxious!

*What restaurants do you like?*

We enjoy Vincent's, Tomaso's, and Windows on the Green at The

Phoenician; I took my granddaughters to breakfast there recently. Also, The Hacienda at the Scottsdale Princess. Those places with a special environment I appreciate very, very much. We sometimes call over to the Olive Garden and I'll bring lasagna and salads home, where we'll watch TV and have a nice meal. We're sort of TV people. We feel a certain guilt about it but it's a fact. We like to relax with a drink and watch TV, especially Tom Brokaw, Larry King, and Seinfeld. Also Charles Grodin: when his opinion coincides with ours, we just love it.

*What was your peak dining experience?*

We've done a lot of traveling, and we've eaten in some elegant places, sometimes when, sensibly, we couldn't afford it. I think the food in France is almost always superb. But I remember well the dinner we had at Tours D'Argent in Paris many years ago. The pressed duck was wonderful, and the view of Notre Dame was spectacular. Another time we had one of those delightful afternoons when we had lunch at a lovely old villa in Sentra, Portugal.

*What should your tombstone say?*

"He lived well, he ate well, and he was blessed with talent." It sounds self-serving, but I don't mean it that way. It's just that I'm eternally thankful for this ability to make a living doing what I love to do.

---

## LOUISE'S BEEF STEW

1 pound stew meat, cut into ½-inch chunks
1 small onion, chopped
2 cloves garlic, minced
2 (10½-ounce) cans beef broth
½ cup water
3 carrots, chopped
1 stalk celery, chopped
½ teaspoon lemon pepper
¼ cup fresh parsley
1 (16-ounce) can diced tomatoes
1½ cups potatoes, cubed (optional)

*"This isn't very glamorous," says Louise McCall. "You just throw all this in together and cook it on medium heat a couple of hours, and serve it with French bread. It serves 4, so if it's just us, there's plenty for the next day, when it's even better. You can also make it with leftover roast or no meat at all."*

# l McCoy

Al McCoy has been the voice of the Phoenix Suns for twenty-five years. Raised on a farm in Iowa, he moved to Phoenix in 1958 to announce for the Phoenix Giants baseball team. He is the father of three grown sons: "Mike, Jerry, and Jay, all Arizonans, and all expert with the grill." McCoy's wife, Georgia, "is of Armenian heritage so she's a very good cook. On our first date, she made her mother's authentic Shish Kebab, and the rest, as they say, is history."

*What did you eat growing up?*

I was raised on meat and potatoes, vegetables. And Maid-Rites. Iowa has a great tradition of Maid-Rites. There are a couple of Maid-Rites here. It's ground beef, steamed, with spices: not as sloppy as a sloppy joe. "My" Maid-Rite at home was in Ames, down by the railroad.

*What are your favorite foods now?*

I'm a pasta person; I could eat it three times a day. I don't eat much meat. My diet, both at home and on the road, is pasta, seafood, chicken, and once in a great while, meat."

*Where do you and Georgia like to go?*

Milano's, Allegro, Tomaso's, Rosario's and Portofino for northern Italian; Avanti, Christos and Christopher's Bistro for Continental. We also like Durant's, Pink Pony, The Outback, Pizzeria Uno, and Nino's. Our restaurants don't take a back seat to any in the country.

*What's your favorite sinful food?*

Pecan pie, especially when I go to the south.

*What's your all-time peak culinary experience?*

New Year's Eve at Avanti has always been a tradition for me. I bring people from New York here, and they rave about it.

*What would you have for your last meal?*

Pasta Puttanesca with hot Italian bread, a nice salad and a bottle of wine. I'd go with a smile on my face!

## MCCOY'S FAVORITE SHISH KEBAB

½ cup vegetable oil
salt to taste (about ½ teaspoon)
½ teaspoon pepper
1 cup red wine
3 large onions, sliced lengthwise
1 tablespoon oregano
1 (6-pound) leg of lamb, bone, fat and gristle removed, and cut into 1½-inch cubes
3 green bell peppers, cut into large chunks
3 tomatoes (or 15 cherry tomatoes), cut into large chunks

*Mix oil, salt, pepper, wine, onions, and oregano; pour over lamb cubes and refrigerate overnight.*

*Stir well several times. Remove meat from marinade and discard onions. Alternate meat with vegetables on short wooden skewers. Cook over charcoal, turning often until meat is evenly done. Do not overcook.*

*Serves 6.*

# Beth McDonald

BETH McDONALD WITH HER RADIO CO-HOST, BILL AUSTIN

KEZ morning personality Beth McDonald grew up in Fort Wayne, Indiana, and moved to Phoenix in 1980 to join KTAR-AM. After two years, she resigned to have her first child. In 1984, she began work with KLZI, now KEZ, where she has hosted the morning show with Bill Austin since 1990. Austin refers to McDonald as a bouncing hand grenade, and The Arizona Republic gave McDonald the Quickest Wit Award for her zingers.

McDonald is married to Lee Blake, who graduated in 1995 from ASU's College of Law. They live in northeast Phoenix and are parents of Shannon, sixteen; Brennan, thirteen; and Bridget, nine.

*So what'd you eat as a kid?*

Ours was a meat-and-potatoes household. Roasts, chicken, meat loaf. Both my parents cooked. My dad's specialty was fried chicken. We had no shortage of fats, growing up.

*When did you first cook?*

My mother's mother and aunt had a restaurant in Paulding, Ohio: Geha's Restaurant, where my great-grandmother had been known for her pies. The thought of them still brings a tear to my dad's eye. So I learned baking first. Mixing and testing. I'm a real good mixer.

*What do you cook now?*

I like to do simple things—pasta, chicken, hamburger. Last night I mixed a pound and a half of ground beef with a little fennel, garlic pepper, onion powder, and red wine. Sometimes I'll marinate chicken with white wine, lemon juice, garlic. I love garlic—isn't it one of the food groups they just added to the pyramid?

*Have a favorite fast food?*

Boston Market! Their side dishes are so good, and they have nice children's items.

*What's your favorite sinful food?*

Fudge cake. I love chocolate, period. I can't tell you how much I love chocolate. Thanks to chocolate, I'm just now losing the weight I gained when I was pregnant with my last baby, and she's now nine.

*Any food you hate?*

Canned creamed corn. Even the smell makes me gag.

*Where do you like to eat out?*

Maria's When in Naples. I love her butternut squash ravioli. Also P. F. Chang's, Z Téjas, Greekfest, Marco Polo, Uncle Sam's for great pizza, Eddie's Grill, Vincent's, Houston's, and—for Irish food—The Black Rose, where I like to sit under the picture of President Kennedy.

*What was the best meal of your life?*

It was in Newport Beach. My husband had surprised me with this trip, and we had a very romantic dinner at The Rex, with the ocean stretching out in front of us. A steak of some kind, and a good wine . . . hmm. People are going to send me AA flyers, but I've made no secret of the fact that I love wine, especially cabernets.

## SOUTHWESTERN BLACK BEAN SALAD

2 (15-ounce) cans black beans, rinsed and drained
1 cup white corn, thawed
1 red bell pepper or half a yellow pepper, diced
⅛ cup red wine vinegar
½ cup olive oil
1 large clove garlic, crushed
5 green onions, chopped
¼ cup chopped fresh cilantro
⅛ teaspoon cayenne pepper
⅛ to ¼ teaspoon cumin (to taste)
½ teaspoon salt
¼ teaspoon pepper

*Combine all the ingredients and refrigerate. You can serve it within an hour or the next day. It's pretty, goes with anything, and is easy, which makes it even better.*
*Serves 8 to 10 as a side dish.*

# Dorothy McGuire Williamson

Dorothy McGuire Williamson grew up in Ohio, where she and her sisters, Christine and Phyllis, "sang in the church choir, and for weddings, funerals, you name it: we sang at the drop of a hat."

The McGuire Sisters got their start in the early 1950s on the Arthur Godfrey Talent Show where they performed for six years. Their first big hit was "Good Night, Sweetheart," followed by "Sincerely," which topped the record charts for twenty-one weeks in 1955.

Williamson and her husband, Lowell, and their family have lived in Scottsdale since 1975. She joins her sisters on the road for occasional gigs, including a recent packed house at the Sun Dome in Sun City.

**How did you learn to cook?**

Our mother was an excellent cook, and we always had our own garden. As a family we canned every summer; I remember sitting on the back porch to snap peas. She had the most beautiful fruit cellar with the jars of jams, jellies, and preserves all lined up. It was fabulous. Each Sunday after church, one of us would fix dinner for everyone.

**What's your favorite fast food?**

I love pizza, and I'm totally addicted to pasta. We must have it three times a week. I used to think it was so fattening but I always get the tomato-basil sauce, which isn't fattening at all. I read somewhere that Vanna White lost all the weight after her baby by eating pasta.

**How do you manage to be the same size you were forty years ago?**

I really get into salads, and fruit. Some days I just have fruit and low-cal cottage cheese. And I run two miles on my treadmill every day. If I don't do it every day, I feel so guilty.

**Do you hate any food?**

You know what? There's not one food I don't like. Well, liver and kidneys I'm not that crazy about.

**Any food weaknesses?**

I love blinis with sour cream and caviar. And for dessert, Vincent's crème brûlée. We go there at least two to three times a month. He always takes good care of us.

**Ever have any cooking disasters?**

One time when we were living in Calgary years ago, I decided to make a little turkey and gravy on my housekeeper's day off. I added too much flour, and by the time I got that gravy thinned down, I must have had gallons of it.

**What's your all-time peak culinary experience?**

One of the best was when the sisters and some friends went to the Mirabelle in London eleven years ago, and in 1994 when Phyllis had a sit-down party for three hundred people at her home in Las Vegas as part of Lee Iacocca's retirement celebration. It was fabulous.

But I think I enjoy most Thanksgiving time with my own family, and all five of my grandchildren. It takes more than food, it takes laughter and love. To me, that's a great experience.

**What should your tombstone say?**

"More, please."

---

### DOROTHY MCGUIRE'S BROCCOLI PASTA

*"This is a taste thrill, believe me. I'm salivating just giving you the recipe."*

16 ounces linguine
1 medium bunch broccoli, cut into
  1-inch pieces (about 6 cups)
¾ cup coarsely chopped walnuts
4 tablespoons (½ stick) butter or
  margarine
1 pint cherry tomatoes, stemmed
1 large clove garlic, minced
½ teaspoon salt
1 pinch red pepper flakes
1 teaspoon dried basil, crumbled
2 tablespoons olive oil
1½ cups (about 1 13¾-ounce can)
  chicken broth
¼ cup chopped fresh parsley
½ cup freshly grated Parmesan
  cheese

*In a large pot, cook the pasta in boiling salted water, adding the broccoli during the last 5 minutes. Meanwhile, toast the walnuts on an ungreased cookie sheet in 350°F for 5 minutes.*

*Melt two tablespoons of the butter in a large skillet. Add the cherry tomatoes, stirring often until just tender. Stir in the garlic, salt, pepper flakes, and basil, cooking 2 minutes on low.*

*Drain the pasta and return to the pot. Add the olive oil and the remaining butter, toss, then add the tomatoes, broth, parsley, and half the cheese. Sprinkle the nuts and the remaining cheese on top.*

*Serves 4.*

# Pat McMahon

KTAR radio host Pat McMahon grew up backstage, the son of vaudevillians Adelaide and Jack McMahon; by the time he was fourteen, Pat had traveled to fifty states and twenty-two countries. A Phoenix media personality since 1960, he started at KPHO-TV as "the guy who does news, weather, farm reports, whatever," and later became the third banana, playing "Gerald" and "Aunt Maude," among other characters, on The Wallace & Ladmo Show, the longest-running children's show in the country.

The father of four grown children, McMahon and his wife, Duffy, live in the Squaw Peak area and travel extensively. Both are passionate about food and wine, says McMahon. "Are you kidding? I get excited about Jell-O."

DUFFY AND PAT McMAHON CLOWN IT UP AT HOME.

90

*Do you cook at home?*

Are you talking about my love life, or are you referring to the kitchen? Actually, I grew up learning the delights of epicurism. My mother was an extraordinary chef, making every kind of exotic ethnic food from recipes she picked up all over the world. My wife is an excellent cook as well. But I've never learned to prepare anything.

*What's your favorite food?*

The first dish I think of is a curried saffron shrimp on a bed of rice that my mother made. I've always had an affinity for shrimp because it's been a nickname of mine for as long as I can remember.

*What's your favorite healthful food?*

I love vegetables and fruits. Anything healthful as long as it isn't from a health food store.

*Your favorite sinful food?*

If you have two long tables, pasta dishes on one side, sweets of the century on the other, I'll head for the pasta. Sweets I can take or leave. Except for Tiramisù. I used to go with her in high school and feel a loyalty even now.

*What food do you hate?*

None. Except oysters, because I die. They sent me to an emergency room in San Francisco once because someone slipped an oyster into my bouillabaisse.

*What was your most memorable dining experience?*

Girardet's. When I went to cover the Reagan/Gorbachev Summit Conference in Geneva, Duffy and I managed to get lunch reservations at this place that is considered to be the number-one restaurant in the world. We took a train from Geneva to Lausanne and a taxi to Girardet's, in this charming house in the middle of this small village outside Lausanne, where we had lunch for three hours. It was spectacular. The cheese board alone probably had 150 choices. Halfway through lunch, big flakes of snow started to fall, and we went back to Geneva on the train with snow falling outside our window.

The next closest thing I can think of is Los Dos Molinos on South Central. And my other favorite thing is potluck. A couple times a year at KTAR, we all bring something in and it's wonderful to sample the rich diversity of food.

*What's the best thing Duffy cooks?*

Everyone says it's her macaroons. But she won't tell anyone how she makes them. Vincent has crawled to the table on his little French knees begging for the recipe. She makes them in the dark: That's how serious she is about nobody finding out what's in them.

*What would your last meal be?*

Very long. I would want one of those suckers that's a progressive meal so they couldn't catch up with me.

## SHRIMP PASTA SALAD

*"Duffy makes this up for me if she's leaving town and I eat it for days. It's one of those things you go back and visit often."*

**VINAIGRETTE:**
¾ cup canola oil
¼ cup balsamic vinegar
¼ cup water
Salt, pepper, lemon pepper, and
   garlic salt to taste

**SALAD:**
16 ounces tricolor spiral pasta
1 pound large fresh shrimp, peeled
½ cup diced celery
½ cup diced onion
½ cup each diced red, green, and
   yellow bell peppers
½ cup peas
½ cup diced sharp cheddar cheese
½ cup sliced artichoke hearts
1 (6-ounce) can whole black olives
2 (4-ounce) cans diced pimientos

*Combine the vinaigrette ingredients in a jar; cover, shake well, and set aside.*

*Cook and drain the pasta. Meanwhile, cook the shrimp in boiling, salted water, just until pink. In a large bowl, combine the pasta, shrimp, and the remaining ingredients, mixing in the dressing at the end.*

*Make early in the day, or the night before serving. Refrigerate. Keeps well, covered, for 4 to 5 days.*

*Serves 12 or more as a side dish.*

# d Mell

Artist Ed Mell is that rarity, a Phoenix native. After graduating from North High and Phoenix College, he earned a degree in advertising and design at Art Center College of Los Angeles. From there he went to New York, where he became art director at a large advertising agency, designing ads for Tang, Fabergé, Air France, Esquire magazine, and covers for National Lampoon.

Since 1978, he has painted images of the West in a style inspired by art deco, cubism, pop art, and the Bauhaus movement, with the purity and vision of Maynard Dixon, Frank Lloyd Wright, and Georgia O'Keeffe. His collectors have included Arnold Schwarzenegger, Barbara and Craig Barrett, the Phoenix Art Museum, and Bill and Erma Bombeck.

Beyond the Visible Terrain: The Art of Ed Mell, by Donald J. Hagerty, was published in 1996 by Northland Publishing.

Mell lives in northeast Phoenix with his sons, Carter and Taylor. His studio is in the Country Club Park area near North High School.

*What did you eat as a kid?*

My mom was a very good cook. She made pot roast, meat loaf, chicken, steaks, and more vegetables than I liked. The vegetables were kind of fifties vegetables . . . brussels sprouts, lima beans, succotash.

*What's the first thing you cooked?*

Oh, you know, macaroni and cheese. Chef Boyardee spaghetti.

*Ever have any cooking disasters?*

In a way. My brother, Frank, and I were always complaining about what we were having for dinner so one night my folks said, go make your own dinner. Frank was about ten and I was six, and at that time, I didn't like hamburgers so of course Frank made hamburgers. My mom and dad were in the next room, eating and listening to us, and we could hear them giggling. Mom says that when it came time for dessert, we went in the dining room and very meekly asked if we could have some.

*Your lunches with artist friends are a tradition. Where do you go?*

I cherish my lunches.

I take a break from my studio and get together with my friends, most of them artists who have studios nearby.

We try to stay within a three-mile radius of our work. We go to Miracle Mile, the Middle Eastern Bakery, Eliana's, Adrian's Mexican Food, or Durant's. The group varies but it includes John Kleber, Kevin Irvin, Jim Cherry, Bob Boze Bell, Cliff Sarde, and Kent Usry. We always have a great time. It's usually a combination of sports analysis and art assessment. Definitely humorous.

*What are your favorite restaurants for dinner?*

Rancho Pinot, Pizzeria Bianco, Eddie's Grill, Mikado, and Havana Cafe.

*What was your peak dining experience?*

There was a great restaurant in Scottsdale when I was a kid. Tico Taco, owned by Waldo Contreras. It's right where the Doubletree Inn is now, near the Scottsdale Center for the Arts. In the early '50s, the area was a little barrio with dirt streets. I can remember riding out there in the back of my dad's 1949 Buick station wagon. We got these great sopapillas there, served with a light, mild chocolate sauce. I heard his secret was peanut oil.

Another peak experience is anytime my mother makes this chocolate cake.

## GERT'S CHOCOLATE CAKE

**CAKE:**
¼ cup canola oil
3 heaping tablespoons cocoa
1 egg
1 cup sugar
1 cup flour
1 teaspoon baking soda
1 cup buttermilk
1 teaspoon vanilla extract

**FROSTING:**
1 square unsweetened chocolate
2 tablespoons butter
2 tablespoons heavy cream
1 heaping cup powdered sugar

*Preheat the oven to 350°F.*

*To make cake, mix the oil and cocoa in a small bowl and set aside. Mix the egg and sugar in a medium-size bowl. Gradually add the cocoa mixture, alternating with the buttermilk, and beating with an electric mixer. Add the baking soda and gradually add the flour. Add the vanilla. Pour into a greased, 8-inch square baking pan and bake for 30 to 35 minutes.*

*Meanwhile, prepare the frosting. Melt the chocolate and the butter in a double boiler. Remove from the heat and add the cream and sugar, beating by hand until smooth. Set back over the simmering water for 10 minutes. Spread immediately over the warm cake.*

*Serves 8.*

# Ann Miller

Film star Ann Miller got her start in show business at age six when she met the famed Bill Bojangles Robinson. "My mother took me backstage after he performed at the Majestic Theater in Houston, and he showed me a tap step." He said, "This little girl is going to be a great tap dancer."

Born in Texas, she moved with her mother to California; to help support the two of them she began dancing professionally when she was eleven (she told the club owner she was eighteen).

She signed with RKO, and made her film debut in 1937, dancing in five Hollywood musicals before heading to New York to dance on Broadway in George White's Scandals of 1939, which had the Three Stooges among its attractions. Forty film musicals later, she returned to Broadway to star in Mame in 1969, and ten years after that, toured with Mickey Rooney in Sugar Babies.

Married briefly three times, she had many famous admirers, including Conrad Hilton and Howard Hughes.

The past few years she has helped lead an effort to save the Orpheum Theatre in downtown Phoenix, where she had danced in the 1940s.

She lives among the red rocks of Sedona with her dogs, Angel and Koko.

*What did you eat as a child?*

A maid would cook or my mother would cook. I have never cooked in my life; I'm not lying. I don't know how to open a can. If my maid got sick, I could starve to death. I'm going to have to learn how to cook someday. If I do decide to cook, I'll go study at Cordon Bleu.

*What do you like to eat now?*

I'm a Texan so of course I like chili, black-eyed peas, fresh corn, banana squash with brown sugar, corn bread, and vegetables cooked with salt pork and onions. I also eat fried chicken when nobody's looking. My problem is, I love to eat. Tex-Mex, Chinese, Mexican, Italian. Oh, yes, I really love Italian. This is a universal stomach here.

*Everyone in Sedona seems to know you because you frequent so many of the restaurants. What are your favorites?*

Here's my routine. I don't eat much for breakfast, and I have a normal lunch, then at dinner I really stuff my face, including a great dessert. I don't think you can beat Shughrue's Hillside; chef Michael Mullins's escargot is to die for and his paella is superb. And I love Renee's, L'Auberge, Joey's, Steak & Sticks, Doll and DeLuca. Judy's is wonderful, too; she'll bake a garlic-rosemary-sage chicken for me that's out of this world. Judy's is like my home.

In Phoenix, I love Vincent's, Mancuso's, The Phoenician—and Mr. C's has superb Chinese cuisine. I also like Christopher's for lunch.

*What are your favorite sweets?*

I love crème brûlée, tiramisù, hot pecan pie with whipped cream, lemon meringue pie, chocolate cream pie. And chocolates? I just had six chocolates while watching TV. You have to watch me around See's Chocolates. I'm just a mess!

*What was the best meal of your life?*

It had to be at Tours d'Argent. I used to date Claude Terrail, the owner. I adore French food, and I had the greatest French dinner in this magnificent restaurant that overlooks the Seine. I wore this black-knit dress the whole time I was there because it expanded. And I had, too.

*Your volunteer work with the Orpheum is appreciated by those of us who care about historic preservation. How did you become involved?*

I was heartsick when they were thinking of demolishing it. It's just awful when real-estate developers destroy something historic so they can build their tacky old modern buildings that look like giant egg crates! The only thing I have in common with Prince Charles is his love of the traditional buildings. So I decided to do all I could to help save the Orpheum.

## TEX-MEX CHILI

*from chef Michael Mullins of Shughrue's Hillside, Sedona*

¼ cup pork fat or vegetable oil
4 pounds lean beef cut into ¾-inch cubes
2 tablespoons flour
8 cloves garlic, minced
6 yellow onions, sliced
5 fresh jalapeños, seeded and minced
4 cups about 2 (10½-ounce cans) beef broth
12 ounces beer (Pearl or Lone Star is best)
2 teaspoons salt
1 teaspoon black pepper
1 tablespoon oregano
2 bay leaves
½ cup red chile paste
2 cups pinto or black beans, cooked and drained
2 tablespoons cornstarch blended with 1 tablespoon white wine vinegar

*Heat the fat in a large skillet; dredge the beef in the flour and fry until brown on all sides. Do not crowd in the pan. Set aside.*

*In a large pot, sauté the garlic and onions; add the jalapeños, beef broth, beer, salt, pepper, oregano, bay leaves, and chile paste. Stir and add the beef. Cover and bring to a boil. Reduce the heat and simmer about 2 hours, stirring often.*

*When the beef is tender; add the beans and the cornstarch mixture. Remove the bay leaves.*

*Serves 8.*

# Jim Mitchum

Courtesy of Jim Mitchum

Actor Jim Mitchum moved to Paradise Valley from Santa Barbara in 1985. He runs the twelve-acre, quarter-horse farm owned by his parents, Robert and Dorothy Mitchum, flying to Hollywood when film projects develop. Saturdays are spent with his children: Price, eight, and Caitlin, seven. His son, Spence, and stepdaughter, Tiffany, live in California.

Mitchum grew up in Los Angeles and remembers when there were no freeways, just trolley cars. As a youngster, he went to Canyon School in Santa Monica and Harvard Military Academy, returning to attend University High in West Los Angeles. There, classmates included Jan and Dean, the Beach Boys, and Nancy Sinatra.

He began acting when he was seventeen, playing a small role in Thunder Road, starring his father. After that, he did "a bunch of kids' movies," in which he was a surfer, later appearing in The Beat Generation in 1961. He played the lead in Track Down in the mid-1970s, and went to China two years ago to film Genghis Khan with Charlton Heston, a TV mini-series that has not been released in the United States.

"I enjoy acting," he says. "But it would be nice if it didn't take so long to set up each scene. So much time is squandered on indecision that the actors are rushed to get their work done. This has always amazed me because the actors' work is all you're left with at the end of the day."

*What did you eat as a kid?*

The basic American food: pork chops, roasts. My mom didn't like to cook but she did cook, and most of the time, we had live-in housekeepers who cooked.

*What do you eat now?*

I've cut out starches and fruit juices, and I'm eating more green vegetables and protein. It's The Zone, where you maintain a ratio of protein to fat.

*What restaurants do you go to?*

The kids like Fuddruckers because they get to build their own hamburgers. Good place, bad name. I go to Oaxaca, Los Dos Molinos, Pischke's, Richardson's, and I like to drive out to Rock Springs for breakfast some Sundays; I also like their pies. I like Avanti's in Scottsdale, When in Naples, Salute, Such Is Life, and Christopher's place on Lincoln, Arizona Grill: we call it The Grill on the Hill.

*What was your all-time peak dining experience?*

I had a whole month of great meals when Angelo Livi and I went to an international television festival in Italy with my father. I'm talking food beyond your imagination.

*What was the best location food you've had?*

That was in the south of France, when my dad was making a movie. On this set, you didn't really work until after lunch. You go to work at 11 A.M. and they have the tablecloths set up for lunch. Then they shoot from one till eight. That was cool.

## DUKE WAYNE'S TAMALE PIE

½ pound pork sausage
2 pounds lean ground beef
1 clove garlic, minced
1 cup chopped onion
1 cup chopped green bell pepper
1 cup chopped celery
2 (16-ounce) cans whole tomatoes
2 cups (about 2 11-ounce cans) whole-kernel corn (Green Giant Mexicorn is best)
1 teaspoon salt
2 tablespoons chili powder
½ cup cornmeal
1½ cups (about 1 6-ounce can) whole black olives
2 cups grated cheddar cheese

*In a large pan, cook the sausage until lightly browned; drain. Add the beef; cook and stir until brown. Add the garlic, onion, green pepper, and celery and cook until onions are translucent. Add the tomatoes, corn, salt, and chili powder. Boil slowly about 15 minutes. Slowly stir in the cornmeal until thickened. Stir in the olives.*

*Preheat the oven to 250°F.*

*Turn the mixture into a large, greased casserole. Top with the cheese and bake for 45 minutes.*

*Serves 8 to 10.*

# Rose Mofford

Former governor Rose Mofford thrived in Arizona politics for more than half a century, from the day she was hired as a secretary to the state treasurer in 1941, after winning a national typing contest at age seventeen.

Raised in Globe, where her father worked in a copper mine, Mofford was president of her class throughout high school and gave the valedictory speech at graduation. A noted athlete, she played basketball and was an All-American in softball, playing for the Globe Cantaloupe Queens.

Mofford was appointed secretary of state in 1977, and became governor when Evan Mecham was impeached in 1987. Known for her selflessness and sense of humor, she has literally hundreds of friends statewide.

Since retirement, Mofford has been active in charitable causes, especially those involving children and the homeless. She collects clothing for those who need it, and distributes it to groups such as Casa de Los Niños and St. Vincent de Paul.

In 1995, she introduced Rose's Salsa, a fat- and cholesterol-free salsa now sold at AJ's, Bashas', and other Arizona stores. All proceeds from the sale of Rose's Salsa go to such organizations as Arizona Save-A-Life Alliance.

*What did you eat as a child?*

My folks were Austrian, and my mother was a wonderful cook. When my parents got married, my mother had a boarding-house with twenty-eight boarders who paid her thirty dollars a month to live there. That included cooking their breakfast and supper and packing their lunch, and washing and ironing their clothes. I'll never forget the great big loaves of bread she would bake.

After she married my father, they had six children—a child every year—and she cooked everything from scratch for all of us. She could make a meal fit for a king out of anything in the icebox.

*Do you cook?*

Let's put it this way. I have a brand-new stove, which I had put in twenty years ago. When this place is sold, the ad could say, "A new stove that's never been used by a little old lady from Globe."

*Ever have any cooking disasters?*

I almost burned down my cabin in Prescott one time when I was making fried walnuts. You cook them in butter and sprinkle them with sugar, and I was cooking with gas, which flamed up.

*Where do you like to eat?*

I like El Bravo, Carlos O'Brien's, the Beef Eaters, Christos, and if I'm real hungry, TexAz Grill. They're very hospitable there. When I go to the racetrack, I'll go to Monti's [La Casa Vieja].

*Any sinful foods you like?*

I have a sweet tooth, and I used to make candy but I leave it alone now. You know why? It all goes to the hips.

*We've heard you have some good recipes. Feel like sharing?*

Oh, I'll share any of my recipes. Anyone who wants one can call me. I'm in the book. I don't have a fax but I do answer all my calls.

## ROSE'S DIVINITY

*"People say it's very good!"*

3 cups sugar
1 cup light corn syrup
¼ teaspoon salt
2 egg whites
1 teaspoon vanilla extract
¾ cup chopped pecans

*Combine the sugar, corn syrup, and salt in an eight-cup saucepan. Bring to a boil and continue cooking without stirring until a little dropped into cold water forms a hard ball.*

*Meanwhile, beat the egg whites until stiff, gradually beating in the hot syrup. Continue beating until the mixture stiffens; add the vanilla and the pecans. Drop by tablespoons onto waxed paper. Let cool.*

*Makes about 40 to 50 pieces.*

# $\mathcal{S}$am Moore

*Mr. Soul Man himself, Sam Moore of Sam & Dave was named to the Rock & Roll Hall of Fame in 1992. An indelible part of the soul era in rhythm and blues, the duo's "Soul Man" sold a million copies and hit number two on Billboard's top singles chart in 1967. A native of Miami, Moore and late partner David Prater formed their act in the 1950s, later recording for Atlantic at the legendary Stax studio, with Isaac Hayes producing.*

*Moore moved to Arizona in 1987 with his wife and manager, Joyce McRae. Moore recently sang background on a Don Henley album and performed with Phil Collins during Atlantic Records' fortieth anniversary concert.*

*What was your childhood like?*

I started singing in the church choir, as my peers did, at the Primitive Baptist Church. I was eleven when I sang my first solo. I saw all those people out there and I just freaked. I forgot the words. I wanted to cry. I wanted to go to the bathroom. I started talking, almost preaching. My grandmother, poor baby, was so embarrassed. She was a real fat lady and she got to sweating so much that her hair came undone, her handkerchief was wringing wet, and her glasses steamed up! People teased me about that for years. I'd say, "I don't want to talk about it."

I was an only child and kind of spoiled. My mother taught school so my grandmother cooked for us. You could take her biscuits and play baseball with them. We lived twenty feet away from the church, and the preacher would be invited to eat with us very often. I hated it when he came. He would eat everything, leaving us with just the chicken foot. I was a little smidgen then, nothing but eyes, but I had a big mouth. Once, when the preacher was there, eating and smacking and sweating and belching, bones flying all out of his mouth, I said, "Why don't you go eat at your house?"

*When did you learn to cook?*

The first thing I cooked, I messed up. I came home from school one day and decided to make me some pancakes. I thought I remembered what my grandmother put in hers. So I put in flour, canned milk, a quart of buttermilk, some grease, and four or five eggs, shells and all. They were beautiful and golden but they were terrible. The dog wouldn't even eat them, and he ate everything.

*Do you enjoy Joyce's cooking?*

She's a wonderful cook. She used to cook and I would just sit there and eat and eat and eat. Pork chops. Pot roast. French toast. Apple pancakes. Spaghetti and meat sauce. I went from 121 pounds to 220. I was so fat, I was nothing but behind and belly. I have to watch very carefully what I eat now. Count my calories.

*What was the best meal of your life?*

Talking about favorite food makes me think of Bruce Springsteen. One time, I was recording with him and we were in the studio, and he had a slice of bread. Now, this is the Boss, right? He's got peanut butter and jelly on the bread, and he's eating it, and he's got jelly coming down his arm and it lands on his shoe. I'm thinking, this man is worth some $200 million, and he isn't eating no cuisine. Made me really like Bruce.

*You're constantly being honored as the artist you are. Do you enjoy those ceremonies?*

Oh, sure. You're rubbing elbows with your peers that you ordinarily wouldn't rub elbows with. But they have all these cold finger sandwiches backstage. I haven't found the food all that delightful at awards shows.

## JOYCE'S CORN-BREAD STUFFING

2 (8½-ounce) packages Jiffy corn muffin mix
1 6-ounce package Pepperidge Farms seasoned croutons
2 pounds chicken livers
2 (12-ounce) packages Jimmy Dean's sage pork sausage
1 (8-ounce) can sliced water chestnuts, drained
1 stalk celery, chopped
1 teaspoon Lawry's seasoned salt
1 teaspoon poultry seasoning
¼ teaspoon Jane's Crazy Mixed-up Pepper
¼ teaspoon paprika
¼ teaspoon rubbed sage
¼ teaspoon garlic powder
1 to 2 (13¾-ounce) cans reduced sodium chicken broth
1 (20- to 22-pound) turkey

*Bake the corn bread according to package directions and let cool. In a food processor, grind separately the corn bread and then the croutons to crumbs. Dump both into a large pot and set aside.*

*Brown the livers and sausage together in a frying pan. Drain the liquid, and set it aside. Grind the meat in the food processor (don't overgrind, as it can get too juicy), and dump it in with the crumbs. Chop separately in the food processor the water chestnuts and then the celery. Add them to the pot.*

*Preheat oven to 325°F.*

*Add the seasonings and the drained meat juice and enough chicken broth to moisten thoroughly. Stuff lightly into the turkey. Bake for 4 hours.*

*Serves 10 to 12.*

# ute Olson

*University of Arizona basketball coach Lute Olson is one of the winningest coaches in Arizona history, with 316 wins since he joined the team in 1983. Named PAC-10 Coach of the Year five times, he made history in 1997 when he led his wildcats to an 84–79 win over Kentucky for the first-ever NCAA championship.*

*Born on a farm near Mayville, North Dakota, he and his wife, Bobbi, live in Tucson. They have five children and eleven grandchildren. Olson was named "Father of the Year" by the Father's Day Council in 1995.*

*What did you eat while growing up?*

I'm Scandinavian and Norwegian. We had hearty meals like pork chops, meat loaf, chicken, mashed potatoes and gravy. We had lutefisk only at Christmas, thank goodness. My mother was home all the time, and there were four kids.

*What foods do you like now?*

I was raised in a generation where you ate what was put on the table, so I developed a taste for most foods. I like seafood. My favorite fish is salmon or halibut, and I like shrimp and steamed clams. I may have a steak or Mexican food every couple of weeks.

*What are your favorite healthful foods?*

I stick very religiously to light foods. If I have lunch, it's very light, usually a big fruit plate, and Boston Market has a good selection of vegetables.

*Have any downfall foods?*

Used to be, I loved ice cream as kind of a treat before you go to bed. But now that I'm trying to stay away from fats, when I get an urge for something sweet, I'll grab an apple or some of Miss Karen's nonfat yogurt. Chocolate-Vanilla Swirl's my favorite.

*Are there any foods you hate?*

When we were on the farm, pigs' feet was one of the delicacies I couldn't stand. My mother and grandfather were accustomed to them but it was not for me.

*What is your peak dining experience?*

Lobster at The Palm, when we play UCLA or USC.

*What are your favorite restaurants?*

Bobbi's a very good cook so we prefer eating at home. Four of our five kids live in town; when it's not the dead of winter, we'll barbecue chicken or fish. When we go out, we like Sakura, El Saguarito, and La Rendezvous.

## BOBBI'S APPLE PANCAKES

*"I use it for recruits," says Bobbi Olson. "They love it, and want their mothers to have the recipe. I always say, 'You can get the recipe if you come here to play.'"*

**BATTER:**
2 medium-size green apples, (Jonathan or Granny Smith), peeled, cored, and chopped in a food processor
2 eggs
2 tablespoons sugar
2 tablespoons butter, softened
2 cups evaporated milk
2 cups Bisquick All-Purpose Baking Mix

**CINNAMON SYRUP:**
2 cups light corn syrup
4 cups sugar
1 cup water
1 tablespoon cinnamon
2 cups evaporated milk

*Combine all the syrup ingredients except the milk and bring to a full boil in a medium-size pot. Cook for 2 minutes, stirring constantly. Let cool a full 5 minutes. Add milk, and serve warm.*

*While waiting for the syrup to cool, mix all the batter ingredients in a large bowl. Spoon onto a greased pancake grill or frying pan and cook over medium-high heat.*

*Serves 4.*

# Pete Pearson

To blues man Big Pete Pearson, cooking is the better gig. "You're in complete control", he says. "You don't have to worry about some musician being on time, or showing up at all."

Pearson, of Big Pete Pearson & the Blues Sevilles, was born in Jamaica and grew up in tiny Pflugerville, near Austin, Texas. Raised by his grandparents, he grew up on lots of vegetables, fish, chicken, and fresh rolls every day.

He began singing and playing guitar with gospel groups. "In fact, my first paying job when I was nine was, well, I thought it was going to be in a church but it was in a bar," Pearson says. "We did 'Caledonia,' 'Jelly Roll,' and 'Just Like a Woman.' We thought we were hot but we probably sounded like crap. I made a dollar fifty, and had to hide it in a cigar box under the house.

"It's all been downhill since that first night."

*Your food is well known since you've had restaurants in Phoenix. Did you learn to cook as a child?*

Oh, yes. My grandmother turned me loose in the kitchen when I was seven or eight. I made roast, pies, pork chops, biscuits, and peach cobbler.

*What's the best thing you make now?*

Smothered chicken and corn bread. I could do that with my eyes shut, and it would come out great every time. And my barbecue sauce . . . mmm. There's no better. What's the secret? I think it's me!

*What's your favorite fast food?*

I don't believe in fast food. I don't believe in those big, greasy hamburgers.

*Do you have a favorite healthful food?*

I'm a salad person. I can live on carrots, celery, cucumbers, and collard greens. I'm a rabbit.

*Where do you like to eat out?*

Rawhide, for steak, and the Fortune Cookie for Chinese food.

*What was your all-time peak dining experience?*

The beefsteak with mushroom gravy and fresh green beans at the Four Courts in Durango, Colorado. Just devastating.

*Did you teach your kids to cook?*

Oh, yes. All four of my daughters would stand on a box or chair while they learned. I think my daughter, Barbara, is a better baker than I am.

*What would your last meal be?*

A big ol' catfish with a little potato salad and some Texas toast. And some of my peach cobbler.

---

### BIG PETE'S PEACH COBBLER

2 (29-ounce) cans sliced
   peaches, undrained
¾ cup (1½ sticks) butter
1 teaspoon cinnamon
1½ cups sugar
2 cups flour

*Preheat the oven to 350°F.*
   *Pour the peaches into a 13 x 9-inch baking dish. Chip ¼ stick of the butter over the peaches, then sprinkle the cinnamon on top. In a medium-size bowl, mix the sugar, flour, and 1 stick of butter until you have crumbs. Cover the peach mixture evenly with the crumbs; add the remaining ¼ stick of butter in tiny pieces over the top. Bake for 30 to 40 minutes.*
   *Serves 8 to 10.*

# Valerie Perrine

Valerie Perrine moved to Phoenix at age seven with her parents, Renee and Ken Perrine. Her father was a stockbroker with E. F. Hutton and later owned an irrigation company and a ranch.

Perrine graduated from Camelback High in 1961 and entered the University of Arizona that fall. The following year she left Arizona for Las Vegas where she landed a job as a dancer in the chorus line at the Desert Inn, which later led to a Hollywood audition. By the early 1970s, she was starring in films, and in 1975, walked away with the best actress award at the 1975 Cannes Film Festival for her portrayal of Honey, Lenny Bruce's stripper wife.

"Always a city person," Perrine has lived in London, Rome, and Paris, and now lives in New York, on the upper *east side. "Manhattan is the easiest place in the world to live in. It takes me three minutes to get anywhere for anything."*

---

*What did your mom cook when you were a child?*

My mother never cooked. My mother told me, very early, "Darling, if you never learn how to cook, you'll never have to." She's quite right, too.

*What are your favorite foods now?*

I eat mostly salads. Salads and vegetables. When I'm hungry for something sweet, I'll have an orange, an apple, or frozen grapes. I'm not a food person. I'm happier eating an apple than going to a restaurant.

*Any sinful foods you crave?*

Rarely. When I do, I'll have Häagen Dazs Chocolate Chocolate, Vanilla Swiss Almond, Coffee, or Rum Raisin ice cream. I used to love Peanut Butter Swirl but they quit making it. Mmm, mmm, that was good.

*Did you ever have any cooking disasters?*

I still do. I set my girlfriend's kitchen on fire twice. My mother set my kitchen on fire once. I do not come from a family of great cooks.

*What restaurants do you like?*

Here, I go to Elaine's. When I'm in Phoenix, I like Macayo's quesadillas and bean burros, and just about everything at Avanti's. The owners, Angelo and Patsy Livi, are friends of mine.

*What foods won't you eat?*

Oysters. Why? Look at them!

## VALERIE'S PASTA THING

8 ounces penne pasta
½ pound buffalo mozzarella, cubed
1 large tomato, chopped
¼ cup fresh basil, chopped
2 cloves garlic, minced
5 to 6 arugula leaves
½ teaspoon salt
¼ teaspoon fresh ground pepper
¼ cup freshly grated Parmesan
   cheese

*Cook and drain the pasta. Transfer the pasta to a platter or bowl. Combine everything else and add to the pasta. Mix to coat.*
   *Serves 2.*

# ave Pratt

Dave Pratt, KUPD's longtime morning man, moved to Phoenix in 1979 to attend college after growing up in California, Arizona, and Nevada, living wherever his dad was doing land development. (His father is Lorne Pratt, who developed Fountain Hills and Lake Havasu City for McCulloch Properties.)

Pratt left college in 1981 to join KUPD, where he hosts one of the country's longest-running rock 'n roll morning shows. "I owe everything to [KUPD owner] Bob Melton," he says. "He took a chance on me."

Pratt and his wife, Paula, live in Chandler with their sons, David Jr., three and a half, and Kyle, two.

**What did you eat as a child?**

I started out on formula, moved into soft foods when I was about fifteen, and was heavy into beer by twenty-one. Actually my mentality as a kid was, if it didn't have a drive-through, I didn't eat there. But my mom expected us to have one square meal a day. She was a wonderful cook. In fact she even put out a cookbook awhile back. Her fried chicken is fantastic. And her red chile.

**Did you learn to cook?**

Sure. Toast. And Pop Tarts. I was pretty good, too, except when they'd slip through the grill. Later on, before I got married in 1988, Jiffy Pop was a pretty big night for me.

**Is your wife a good cook?**

Let me put it this way. On a cooking and eating scale, I hit the jackpot. I mean, she's Italian. And her dad's cooking! When we first dated, Paula was a very pretty lady, but after I ate her dad's cooking, she became beautiful. So between my mom and her dad, I'm covered.

**Where do you like to eat out?**

I love the food at Christopher's—you know Chris Gross is a young guy who likes rock and likes to ride motorcycles. He's cool. I also like Guedo's Tacos here in Chandler; Kyoto, Honeybears Barbecue, and I have to mention Durant's because it's so great. I love the food, I love the fact that you walk through the kitchen, and I love the aesthetics—the red velvet wallpaper. Red's my color, you know.

**Any favorite sinful foods?**

Macadamia brittle. My wife makes that over the holidays for friends, when I'm trying to stay in shape for all these appearances I make, and it's over for me.

**What is your peak dining experience?**

Denny's, on my birthday. It was free. Hey, I'm in radio.

---

### PAULA PRATT'S PRETZELS AND BEER

*"First she gives me a beer to get me out of the kitchen."*

1 package dry yeast dissolved in 1½ cups warm water
1 teaspoon salt, plus some to sprinkle on top of pretzels
1 tablespoon sugar
4 cups flour
1 egg

*Preheat the oven to 425° F.*

*Add the salt and sugar to the yeast mixture, then gradually add the flour, kneading as you go. Knead the dough for 5 minutes. Twist, a handful of dough at a time, into pretzel shapes. Place two inches apart on a cookie sheet lined with foil.*

*Beat the egg, and brush some on each pretzel. Sprinkle with salt. Bake for 12 to 15 minutes.*

*Makes 20 pretzels.*

# Francine Reed

Francine Reed grew up in and around Chicago, one of six children who sang all the time. "These little Reed kids and their outfits, Lord! We sang at church, at Kiwanis Club, at home. The biggest thing in our lives was singing together."

She moved to Phoenix in 1973 and began singing professionally with her sister, Margo Reed. "[Former Arizona Republic writer] Pat Myers started the ball rolling in 1974 by writing the first article on us. We bless her for that."

After creating a sensation singing in Phoenix/Scottsdale clubs, Reed was discovered by Lyle Lovett, who asked her to tour and record with his band. Reed now lives in Atlanta, continuing to perform with Lovett and in solo gigs. She records

*for Ichiban Records and has just
released her second CD. When in town,
Reed performs at the Rhythm Room
and at Mesa's Blues Blast.*

*What did you eat, growing up?*

Grits, beans, and rice. Mom was the only
one around to buy food and clothes for
all these kids, but we were never hungry.
It was a wonderful time. We were always
singing.

*When did you learn to cook?*

I didn't cook much when I was little, but
I remember when I got my own little
place in 1970, trying to make pork chops
and gravy for some guy. I put too much
flour in the skillet and it boiled over. Of
course I called Mom. Still do. "How do
you make this?" She doesn't tell you
everything, though. She'll say, "You don't
need to know how to make that, I'll make
it for you."

*What foods do you like now?*

I don't eat a whole heck of a heap different than I ever did except I am cooking
more health conscious now, on account
of I don't want to get any bigger because
I don't want to buy any more clothes! I

don't fry much today. Except I got to fry
me a pork chop now and then. And about
twice a month I have to fry me a chicken,
plain and simple. Once a year I eat trot-
ters and listeners. That's pigs' feet and
pigs' ears.

*Ever stop by a fast-food place?*

No, because I don't drive. I haven't driven
in many years. You know when that law
came along, "Don't drink and drive?"
Honey, I chose drinking. I'm one of
those born wild women who likes to
have a drink when I'm working. So
I quit driving.

*What was your peak dining experience?*

Any meal at Mom's.

*Where do you like to eat out?*

Mexican food's my favorite when I'm in
Phoenix because we don't have anything
you could consider Mexican food in
Atlanta. Andy Gonzales's mom's house is
the best: Carmen Gonzales makes real,
authentic, sho 'nuff Mexican food. I also
like Oaxaca and Ricardo's.

*Hate any foods?*

There was a time I couldn't eat olives. But
I put them in martinis now, and they're
not bad at all.

## FRANCINE'S FABULOUS FRIED CHICKEN

1 teaspoon salt
½ teaspoon pepper
½ teaspoon garlic powder
1 whole chicken, washed, cut up,
   and dried on paper towels
½ cup flour
2 cups corn or safflower oil

*Combine the salt, pepper, and garlic pow-
der, and sprinkle the chicken generously
with the mixture. Put the flour in a
plastic bag; add each piece of chicken, one
at a time, and shake until well coated.*

*Heat the oil in a cast-iron skillet to
425°F. Fry half the chicken until golden
brown. Drain on paper towels while frying the second half. Enjoy!*

*Serves 6.*

# kip Rimsza

*Skip Rimsza was elected Phoenix mayor in 1994 and again in 1995, after serving as District 3 council member since 1990. At age forty-one, he is one of the youngest mayors in Phoenix history.*

*Born in Chicago, Rimsza moved to Phoenix as a small child. As a young man, he and a brother were hunting guides in Alaska. He has been active in real estate for many years, and served as president of the Phoenix Board of Realtors.*

*Mayor Rimsza and his wife, Kim Gill-Rimsza, have five children: Brian, sixteen; Jenny, fifteen; and triplets Alexander, Taylor, and Nicole, two.*

*In his spare time, Rimsza likes to restore old cars and trucks; he drives a restored 1956 Ford pickup.*

*What did you grow up eating?*

I can tell you exactly what we ate. I had seven brothers and sisters, half of them older, half younger. My mother passed away when I was sixteen. Dad would cook a pot roast, and break open a head of lettuce. That was dinner.

*Do you remember what you first cooked?*

No, but I was probably nineteen before I cooked anything. In a big family like ours, the girls did most of the cooking and the boys did the lawn work, plumbing, the cleaning up, and the outside stuff. We took care of the horses and a dairy cow.

*Ever have any cooking disasters?*

Sure. The biggest one was when I was first married. I love to hunt and fish, and I thought I would introduce my wife to some well-prepared javelina. There's no such thing as well-prepared javelina. Remember Crock-Pots? I boned the javelina and cooked it for six or eight hours with barbecue sauce. It tasted great but there were hundreds of tiny bones we had to pick out. In a sandwich it was disaster. To this day, javelina is not even allowed in the freezer.

*What healthful foods do you enjoy?*

I always watch it. I never eat anything but salad or vegetarian at lunch. For dinner, I hold it to fish or skinless chicken; my favorite way is cooked on the grill.

*What food do you hate?*

I know exactly. Ethiopian food. To my palate, it's like little piles of dog food, eaten with little sponges. I had some at The Red Sea in Washington, and it killed me physically. Brutal.

*What food is your downfall?*

Cookies. Lemon bars or oatmeal raisin cookies and a glass of milk. Ooooh.

*What was your peak dining experience?*

When we were newly married, we ate at the Maryland Inn in Anapolis. It's a historic structure with plenty of atmosphere, and the meal was wonderful. I remember we had crab cakes and soft-shell crabs.

*What should your tombstone say?*

"Here he lies. Ate right and died anyway."

## SKIP'S FAVORITE LEMON BARS

½ pound (2 sticks) butter
½ cup powdered sugar
2¼ cup flour, sifted
4 eggs, lightly beaten
4 tablespoons lemon juice
Grated rind of 2 lemons
   (about 4 teaspoons)
2 cups sugar
1 teaspoon baking powder

*Preheat the oven to 350°F.*

*With a fork, cut the butter, powdered sugar, and two cups of the flour together into fine crumbs. Pat into a buttered 13 x 9-inch baking pan. Bake 15 minutes.*

*Meanwhile, combine the eggs with the lemon juice and rind. Sift together the sugar, remaining ¼ cup of flour, and baking powder, and combine with the egg mixture. Pour over the crust and bake 25 minutes.*

*Sprinkle with powdered sugar and let cool. Cut into squares.*

*Makes 20 to 24 pieces.*

# $\mathcal{F}$ritz Scholder

Painter/sculptor Fritz Scholder has received numerous awards in his thirty-seven-year career, including fellowships from the Whitney Foundation, the Rockefeller Foundation, and the Ford Foundation. Best known for his boldly colored canvases depicting the American Indian, Scholder has been the subject of eleven books and two public television programs. His work has been exhibited throughout the United States and in France, Japan, China, Germany, and at the Hermitage Museum in St. Petersburg, Russia.

He recently completed Painting the Paradox, *an hour-long documentary on his life and work filmed in Egypt, Paris, New York, Santa Fe, Sun Valley [Idaho], and Scottsdale. Narrated by* N. Scott Momaday, the film was directed by Paul Perry and shot by Marlin Darrah for International Film and Video.

A native of Minnesota, Scholder grew up in Wahpeton, North Dakota. He has lived in Scottsdale since 1972.

---

*What did you eat as a child?*

My mother liked to make theme dinners. Every Friday night was "Poor Man's Dinner": pig knuckles and bread pudding.

*Do you cook?*

Early on, I was the world's worst cook. All I could fix for my son when he was a pre-schooler was a Scholder Hot Dog or Scholder Soup. The hot dog I burned black on both sides, and the soup a monk taught me to make. You add a can of cold milk to a can of Campbell's Tomato Soup, and eat it with tons of crackers. To this day, if I'm in the studio and don't want to quit painting, I'll rush in and make myself some Scholder Soup.

*Cook any better now?*

Yes. In 1965, one of the greatest cook-books came out. *The Artists and Writers Cookbook* [Angel Island Publications]. Recipes like Steak à la Acetylene. You use the tools you have around the studio.

In 1995, I won a cooking award for my lemon steak recipe at the March of Dimes Gourmet Gala. Actually, Vincent [Guerithault] cooked it. You simply take the best steak you can buy and slice it in thin strips, and sauté it in butter. Squeeze fresh lemon over it and cover it with capers.

*Where do you like to eat out?*

In Paris: There's a great Mexican restaurant called The Studio run by two guys from California. Wherever I go, I search out the thing one should order.

Here, I like Vagara Bistro for their bratwurst or calamari salad. Los Olivos for their cheese crisp and sangrita—it's not sangria, there is a difference. The Tee Pee Tap Room has the world's greatest chile relleno, and AZ 88 has the best buffalo wings in the country. I love Vincent's foie gras, and Windows on the Green's rattlesnake steak. Also P. F. Chang's orange-peel beef. La Parrilla Suiza is a great Mexican café, and I have another that will remain my secret. Only a hint: It's on McDowell in Phoenix, and it's like walking into Mexico.

*What was your peak dining experience?*

That's a toss-up. Between a four-hour lunch at a little place outside Giverny with views of a huge valley, drinking wine from wax-encrusted bottles, and Chinois in Santa Monica. Chinois is one of the best gourmet restaurants in the country. Their French-fried spinach is a must, so light and delicate. Every time I go there is a peak experience.

*Any favorite sinful foods?*

Yes, I'm glad you mentioned it. Fresh truffles sliced over a pile of angel hair pasta. With Kristal champagne and caviar. I have my own truffle slicer. But lots of luck finding truffles in Phoenix.

*I bet you avoid fast foods.*

I love fast foods. McDonald's. KFC. Pizza Hut. I have to have my fix.

*Any foods you hate?*

A couple. I hate lutefisk: It gags me. And anything in Romania is inedible. It's one country where you could truly starve to death. Even an egg, and their bread . . .

*What should your tombstone say?*

"Keep the foie gras warm. I'll be right back."

## GAZPACHO FROM BARCELONA
("Scholder's Liquid Salad")

*"This gazpacho is pink instead of red, and I think it's even more refreshing than Mexican gazpacho."*

1 (32-ounce) jar tomato juice
1 (6-ounce) can tomato paste
1 (8-ounce) can tomato sauce
½ cup olive oil
½ cup white wine vinegar
2 eggs
6 slices white bread
1 tablespoon butter
1 cucumber, peeled and diced
5 green onions, diced
2 tomatoes, diced
1 green bell pepper, diced
½ cup sour cream

*In a large bowl, beat together the tomato juice, paste, and sauce, and the olive oil, vinegar, and eggs with a spoon, mixing thoroughly. Transfer to a serving bowl, cover, and chill several hours.*

*Toast the bread lightly, cut into small squares, and sauté in the butter. Pile in a basket or on a plate.*

*Place the vegetables in separate mounds on a large platter.*

*Ladle the chilled mixture and a big glob of sour cream into each bowl. Serve with the bread, and let everyone help themselves to the vegetables they want in their soup bowl.*

*Serves 6.*

# Doc Severinsen

*Phoenix Symphony principal Pops conductor Doc Severinsen is a part-time Arizonan, appearing here annually over the last fifteen years.*

*Severinsen achieved international fame as* The Tonight Show's *musical director, a position he held for more than thirty years, first with Steve Allen, the last twenty-five with Johnny Carson.*

*A Grammy Award winner, Severinsen has recorded more than thirty albums and CDs.*

*Severinsen was raised in eastern Oregon "where most of the people who had come over the Oregon Trail were from the South."*

*He and his wife, Emily, live in Santa Barbara, where "we have a wood-burning pizza oven just outside the kitchen door."*

*What did you eat growing up?*

What everyone else did. Farm cooking. A little bit of meat, a lot of beans, greens, and potatoes. My father was born in Paris, and his father was an itinerant shoemaker so they had traveled all over Europe. My dad became a dentist in Oregon, and he always had a fantastic garden with beets, collard, turnips, kale. I ate soul food for forty years before I found out what it was. To this day, I love a good mess of green beans with a little pork.

When I was about seventeen, I left home and went on the road, traveling with big bands. Most of the guys I worked with were Italian, and from the first Italian meals I had, I was gone. That changed my life. That's about all we eat at home now.

*Do you cook?*

We both do. If I'm coming home from a road trip, my wife always makes me a pot of brodeto—fish soup. She makes it as good as it can be made. Mostly we eat fish and salad, made after a stroll to the garden to pick what's fresh.

Or I'll start the pizza oven at eight in the morning, have breakfast and start cooking. At ten at night, we're still sitting around the pizza oven.

*Is there anything you hate?*

As a kid, I hated fried parsnips; now I wish I could get some. And creamed turnips. No, I can't think of anything I hate. I'll even eat barbecued cow's head. You pick the meat off the skull and put it in a soft taco.

*What's your favorite indulgence?*

I eat desserts very sparingly, usually a tablespoon of gelato or something. But steak. I don't eat it often but all of a sudden my body tells me to find a good steak.

*Where do you eat in Phoenix?*

I'm a Gold Card member of the Italian American Club here, and I also like El Bravo, the Fish Market, and Mrs. White's Golden Rule Cafe.

*What would your last meal be?*

A simple plate of pasta. My tombstone would say, "He ate well and died happy. And he had a good palate." That's the nicest compliment you can get from an Italian.

*Even better than, "You play a mean horn?"*

That I'm supposed to do. By the way, I know how to get the world straightened out. If everybody would just eat Italian food, there wouldn't be any more wars. All you need is music, love, and Italian food.

## DOC'S PASTA CHI CHI

*"This is great for lunch on a cold winter's day. Pour into bowls, grate fresh Parmesan over the soup, and serve with some good, fresh Italian bread. My kids and grandkids always ask me to make this for them."*

½ cup chopped celery
½ cup sliced carrots
2 tablespoons olive oil
3 cloves garlic, minced
2 cups chicken stock
1 (16-ounce) can garbanzo beans
¼ cup ditilini (tiny, tube-shaped) pasta

*What you do is brown the celery and carrots in the oil, adding the garlic last so it doesn't burn. Put in the stock—use homemade, not canned—and the beans, then add the ditilini, and cook for five minutes.*
*Serves 4.*

# Robert Shields

Robert Shields got his start as San Francisco's first street mime. Discovered by Herb Caen, he teamed with Lorene Yarnell in the 1970s to create Shields & Yarnell, an Emmy Award–winning performance-art nightclub act. The pair toured the world for several years, performing for two U.S. presidents and doing a command performance for the Queen of England. The duo broke up in 1984, and Shields later settled in Sedona, where he and his wife, Rhonda, now live.

Shields has painted and sculpted for most of his life, and now makes art full time. His paintings and jewelry designs are shown at shops in Los Abrigados, Sedona, and at The Phoenician in the Valley.

*What did you eat as a child?*

I grew up in L.A. My dad made matzo-meal pancakes for me, and I also loved melted cheese sandwiches and banana pudding.

*Do you remember the first thing you cooked?*

Bacon. I loved it because it made all sorts of sounds, like little firecrackers.

*Ever have any cooking disasters?*

Once the frying pan caught on fire when I was making French toast, and another time I caught the whole kitchen on fire when I walked into the other room while making popcorn. I burned part of my hand; it was really scary.

*What do you eat now?*

My wife and I eat sparsely; we may have a baked potato and salad for dinner. Last night we had spaghetti squash with garlic and some great olive oil. I love pastas, fish, and chicken. I was a vegetarian for most of my life, but I've always believed you could have one foot in the gutter. Let's say I go to your house and you serve meat loaf. I'll eat it.

I'm actually kind of a snob about food, and wine, too. I never drink wine at most parties because it's not to my taste. The wines I prefer are Cafera Piñot Noir, Kristler Chardonnay, and Martini Ray Cabernet Sauvignon.

*When you really have one foot in the gutter, what do you pig out on?*

An avocado, a lemon, and some fresh chips. I love stuffed grape leaves, too. And goat cheese and Greek olives. Or black beans, cilantro, rice, and chives. I'm getting hungry talking about it.

*What was your peak dining experience?*

I couldn't choose one. I've eaten with Brezhnev in Shanghai, and pasta fagioli with Frank Sinatra—just the two of us—and had fantastic French food with Marcel Marceau when I stayed at his house. I used to have chicken soup with Groucho Marx all the time. We'd eat and watch *Duck Soup* at his house. I had a phenomenal dinner one time in Taipei with the Chinese Mafia. Everything was wonderful: the silver, the china, the table-cloths. I don't even know what I had, but it cost $2,000 a plate and went on for three and a half hours.

*What about sweets?*

I love flan, and Godiva or Ghirardelli chocolate, but I'm very sensitive to all that sugar. My stomach starts hurting.

*What's your favorite place to eat?*

Pietro's in Sedona, owned by Phillip Shivel and Jon Leon. I love an angel hair pasta dish so much they've named it Pasta Shields.

**PASTA SHIELDS**
(from Chef Shivel of Pietro's)

12 ounces capellini pasta
4 cloves garlic, minced
½ cup extra-virgin olive oil
   (the best you can buy)
¾ cup julienned zucchini
¾ cup julienned yellow squash
½ cup minced red onion
¼ cup julienned carrots
¼ cup sliced shitake mushrooms
6 to 8 small leaves purple kale or
   savoy cabbage
⅓ cup sun-dried tomatoes
¼ cup fresh minced basil
¼ cup white wine
¼ cup grated Parmesan cheese
Salt and freshly ground black
   pepper to taste

*Cook and drain the pasta; keep covered.*

*In a large skillet, sauté the garlic in the oil; add the vegetables, tomatoes, and basil, cooking no more than 4 minutes over medium-high heat, stirring constantly. Douse with the wine; cook down 1 or 2 minutes.*

*Add the pasta and toss. Add the cheese and toss again. Sprinkle with salt and pepper.*

*Serves 2.*

# $\mathcal{D}$ebbie Sledge

**LEFT TO RIGHT: DEBBIE, JONI, AND KIM**

Courtesy of World Scope Artists

Sister Sledge—Debbie, Joni, and Kim Sledge—have sung together professionally for twenty years, achieving national fame in 1979 for "We Are Family," a soul anthem that eventually went double platinum. Raised in Philadelphia, they began by singing in church, and were heavily influenced by their grandmother, opera singer Viola Williams.

Deeply religious, Debbie and Joni Sledge continue to perform for church and secular functions nationally and in the Phoenix area, where they now live. (Kim Sledge is married to a Philadelphia surgeon, and flies to meet her sisters for concerts. Baby sister Kathy and older sister Carol spell their famous siblings when needed.)

Sister Sledge starred in the summer '97 Cancun Jazz Festival, and recently recorded a soundtrack for Brother,

*Brother, Stop*, *a play about preventing gang violence.*

*We interviewed Debbie Sledge at the Phoenix home she shares with her husband and six children.*

*What did you eat as kids?*

We were raised by our mom, who was divorced from our father. She and my grandmother were both good cooks. Mom worked but what she made for us was always fast and delicious. Spanish rice. Sausage and peppers. Fresh biscuits. We were rushing all our lives, so she'd make us these nutritious power shakes with yogurt, fresh fruit, and protein powder. She was very knowledgeable about nutrition, really ahead of her time.

*What do you eat now?*

Healthy food was ingrained in all of us. I always loved salads so much, they called me Rabbit. I love taking my kids for salad; we usually go after church. My sister Joni is a gourmet cook, while I'm just a homebody cook. I use something I learned from my mom: When I'm just serving something I made up out of what's in the fridge, I give it an exotic name, like Hungarian goulash.

*What are your sinful foods?*

I'm a chocoholic. It's terrible. I have to have a brownie with chocolate sauce now and then. My husband spoils me with chocolate candy.

*What's been your peak dining experience?*

Oh, goodness, I've had so many wonderful ones. It's the company you're with that makes it special. But last Thanksgiving was an especially blessed time. Twenty-some relatives flew in for a family reunion. We did something special. We lined each of the children up and we blessed each one of them.

## THE BEST SALAD

**SALAD:**
½ head romaine lettuce, torn into
   bite-size pieces
½ head iceberg lettuce, torn into
   bite-size pieces
6–8 spinach leaves, torn into
   bite-size pieces
1 cucumber, peeled and sliced
1 (11-ounce) can mandarin orange
   slices, drained
½ bermuda onion, sliced thin
¼ cup slivered green bell pepper
¼ cup slivered red bell pepper
2 medium-size carrots, peeled and
   grated
1 (12-ounce) can water chestnuts,
   drained and sliced
2 ripe avocados, peeled and sliced

**MOM'S VEGGIE DRESSING:**
½ cup puréed fresh vegetables
   of your choice
2 tablespoons balsamic vinegar
2 tablespoons canola or olive oil
Juice of 1 lemon (about 3 tablespoons)
½ teaspoon sugar
1 teaspoon Lawry's seasoned salt
1 tablespoon chopped fresh basil
   (or 1 teaspoon dried)

*Combine all salad ingredients and combine all ingredients for dressing. Toss together.*
   *Serves 8 to 10.*

# Sam Steiger

Sam Steiger, longtime radio talk-show host, journalist, and resident curmudgeon, is now featured on KUSK and in the Tribune newspapers. He served in the Arizona State Senate for two years, and was a U.S. Congressman for ten years. A Korean War tank platoon leader, he was awarded a Silver Star and a Purple Heart.

Since 1954, he has lived in Prescott, where he's a rancher and horse trader. "My idea of a great vacation is helping someone gather cows," he says.

He achieved local notoriety in 1975 when he shot and killed two burros that he said had attacked him; ironically he resides on Burro Drive in Prescott. In 1986, he boosted his reputation for eccentricity by painting a crosswalk on Montezuma Street in downtown Prescott, connecting the Courthouse

*Square with Whiskey Row, a crosswalk that had been eliminated earlier in the year by the state on liability grounds. It is believed that he and several friends had discussed the matter over cocktails in a Whiskey Row club prior to the infamous painting. (He was later found innocent of defacement charges.)*

*In 1990, he ran for governor and published a best-selling joke book,* Kill the Lawyers *(Prickly Pear Press).*

---

*So, how'd you learn to cook?*

I didn't. I do eggs and bacon, and meat loaf. The microwave saved my life. I was impressed with the man on the moon, but there's no question that the microwave had a greater impact on my own life.

*Your favorite sinful food?*

There is no sinful food. All food is beneficial. If you can eat it, it's good for you. That's the Steiger rule. You may call meat loaf and eggs fried in bacon grease sinful, but I call it an advance in science.

*What's your favorite fast food?*

That's the only culinary line I draw. One of the funniest things I ever saw was McDonald's banning smoking. Anyone who eats at McDonald's obviously has no concern for their health.

*How about your favorite healthful food?*

There is no unhealthy food. The chicken-fried steak at the TexAz Grill is the best in the West.

*Your all-time peak culinary experience?*

It was on a cruise. I was able to consummate the sexual act in a dining room while eating Cherries Jubilee. Yes, the dining room was closed; what do you think I am, decadent?

*Your most hated food?*

I do not dislike any food. However, deep-fried anything is preferable to any salad, but I also like salad. I cherish anchovies, which makes me a social outcast in many circles.

*Any cooking disasters?*

No, everything I cook turns to gold. The secret is, don't cook too often.

*What should your tombstone read?*

"He died fat but happy."

## MEAT LOAF

*"You remember Lyndon Johnson called his dog 'Dog?' Well, this is just 'meat loaf.'"*

1 pound ground veal
1 pound ground beef
1 pound ground pork with a lot of fat
1 (3½-ounce) jar capers, undrained
3 tablespoons mayonnaise
3 eggs
1 cup garlic-flavored bread crumbs
8 cloves fresh garlic (chop the hell out of it)
Pepper and garlic salt to taste
½ cup marmalade
4 slices bacon

*Preheat the oven to 350°F.*

*In a large bowl, combine the meat, capers, mayonnaise, eggs, bread crumbs, garlic, pepper, and garlic salt. Press the mixture into a large glass casserole dish, and spread the marmalade on top. Then arrange the strips of bacon over the marmalade layer. Cook, uncovered, for 1 hour.*

*Serves 10.*

# Ann Symington

Ann Pritzlaff Symington became Arizona's first lady in 1991, when her husband, Fife Symington, was sworn in as governor of Arizona.

A Wisconsin native, she moved to Phoenix with her family in 1958. Her father, John Pritzlaff, Jr., served District 24 in the Arizona House and Senate for fifteen years, and was later named ambassador to Malta by President Nixon.

Symington attended Arcadia High as a freshman, completing high school at Miss Porter's School in Connecticut. "Me and Jackie," she quips. Following college at Scripps College and San Francisco State, she returned to Phoenix and taught second grade in the Washington district.

Married since 1976, she and the governor have five children.

**FIFE AND ANN SYMINGTON**

124

**What did you eat as a child?**

Coming from Wisconsin, we had lots of cheese and butter. Both my parents are great cooks. Dad is great at soup, and my mom still whips up Hollandaise sauce as if it were no problem. Like many families, we had liver once a week.

**What was the first thing you cooked?**

Probably scrambled eggs. Being the oldest, I started to baby-sit my sister and two brothers when I was around twelve. I became very good at heating TV dinners for my siblings.

**Ever have any cooking disasters?**

The worst was probably my first date with Fife. I thought I'd be really cool and make this fondue. Well, as I was carrying the pot of hot oil to the table, the handle came loose and I spilled hot oil down the table and down my front. Fife was very gracious. I probably burst into tears because it hurt. Fortunately, I wasn't really burned.

Other disasters? Oh, burned cookies and pots boiling dry. The things you forget when you're on the phone. The portable phone is a godsend for the kitchen.

**What do you eat now?**

It's pretty much chicken or fish, and I love to make big salads. The kids all like them, too. For the dressing, I just mix a little balsamic vinegar with olive oil and maybe some oregano.

**What are your favorite healthful foods?**

Apples. I really like a good, crisp, cold apple. It can even be better than peanut M&Ms.

**Have any favorite sinful foods?**

Chocolate cake, chocolate anything. I find Vincent's warm chocolate soufflé very satisfying.

**Besides Vincent's on Camelback, what are your favorite restaurants in the Valley?**

Tarbell's, Chianti, Tomaso's, and The News Cafe.

**What was your peak dining experience?**

I've had so many but I guess the first testing dinner before the Ritz Carlton opened has to be among them. It was so exciting as well as so good.

**What should your tombstone say?**

"She came, she cooked, she conquered."

## AUBERGINE

*"When we were in Malta, I spent lots of time in the kitchen watching the chef make many great things, including this dish."*

2 to 3 large, luscious eggplants, peeled and sliced very thin
½ cup olive oil
2 cups homemade (or 2 8-ounce cans) tomato sauce
2 cups fresh grated Parmesan or Romano cheese
6 eggs, beaten

*Preheat the oven to 350°F.*

*Fry the eggplant slices in as little olive oil as possible; blot on paper towels.*

*Cover the bottom of an attractive, deep casserole dish with a thin layer of tomato sauce. Add one layer of eggplant; top with more sauce, and a generous amount of cheese. Spoon half the beaten egg over this. The egg will gravitate to the sides, which is fine, but make sure some remains in the center, as this is the glue that holds the dish together.*

*Continue layering the eggplant, sauce, and cheese, until you have three layers, making sure the top layer is attractive. Prior to baking, lift under and around all the layers with a fork so the egg will settle as it should.*

*Bake for 30 minutes. Serve hot or cold.*

*Serves 10.*

# Marshall Trimble

Humorist/historian Marshall Trimble is the author of fourteen books and one of the most sought-after speakers in the state. An Arizona native, he draws on his childhood in Ashfork in spinning colorful stories. Called "the Will Rogers of Arizona" by radio personality Pat McMahon, he has opened for such acts as Waylon Jennings and Jerry Lee Lewis.

Trimble's popular Arizona History class at Scottsdale Community College averages over a hundred students, and is the largest class on campus.

He lives with his wife, Gena, and son, Roger, in Paradise Valley.

*What did you eat as a kid?*

Ashfork was a wonderful place for a kid to grow up. It had an old-fashioned soda fountain, a picture show, a pool hall, and it even had the Harvey House; what else do you need? My dad was a fireman on the Santa Fe, and my mom was a waitress at the Dew Drop Inn and other places around Ashfork. My brothers and I used to fix rice for breakfast with a little milk and sugar in it. We ate a lot of venison, too. I wouldn't say my dad hunted out of season but we had some mighty funny-looking goats hanging in our barn sometimes. Goats with antlers.

I remember taking a basketball trip one time, and stopping in Flagstaff, where somebody ordered a chicken-fried steak. I'd hardly ever been in a restaurant but I ordered a chicken-fried steak like I'd been ordering them all my life.

*What do you like to eat now?*

I like steak. In fact, my favorite thing is to go to Houston's and have the New York steak with a bottle of merlot. That's about all it takes to really make me happy. 'Course, I'll eat anything that's put in front of me. Even broccoli, which I'll eat once in awhile to please my wife.

*Any foods you can't stand?*

I'll bet I wouldn't like caviar. Isn't that fish eggs? Well, you know what fish do in water. . . . Another thing I don't like is—well, let me tell you about the time I was lost in the mountains north of Ashfork for days with nothing to nibble

on but a bar of soap. To this day, I don't care much for the taste of soap.

*Did you ever have any cooking disasters?*

Oh, sure. The worst was one time when I was making a mock pecan pie with beans instead of pecans for Rita Davenport's cooking show. It left a raunchy smell in the house for three days. I remember that Rita was broadcasting from the state fair, and she was wearing a dress with elastic at the top. Well, the only thing holding Rita's dress up was a city ordinance, and then some child pulled it down. On camera.

*What are your sinful foods?*

Chocolate. I love chocolate. Especially Hershey's with almonds. My wife tries to not keep any around the house but sometimes I go into a fit and roll around on the floor until I get one. But I'll never buy them at the movies. I have a policy about that. I give handouts to those who need it at the time, but I will not give a nickel to someone holding me up. I'd rather throw a five-dollar bill out in the street than buy a candy bar with it.

*What's your all-time peak dining experience?*

Arizona Highways took a bunch of us up to celebrate the Grand Canyon's seventy-fifth anniversary. It had snowed and the canyon has never been so beautiful. We stayed at El Tovar for three days, and I've never had a gourmet experience like that. I ordered steak at every meal. Growing up poor, you order steak every chance you get.

**MARSHALL TRIMBLE'S COWBOY CHILI**

5 pounds javelina, elk, deer, goat meat, or beef, cut into ½-inch cubes
2 cups hot water
½ pound green chiles, peeled and diced
2 tablespoons red chili powder
2 cloves garlic, chopped
1 teaspoon oregano
1 tablespoon cayenne pepper
2 large onions, chopped
1 horseshoe, cleaned

*Combine the meat, water, chiles, chili powder, garlic, oregano, cayenne pepper, and onion in a large cooking pot and bring to a boil. Lower heat and simmer for 1 hour. Drop in horseshoe. If horseshoe sinks, simmer for another hour or until horseshoe rises to the top. If using javelina, this is ready to eat when horseshoe is tender enough to cut.*

*Skim off the grease, and serve. Serves 10.*

# *J*esse Valenzuela

Courtesy of Danny Clinch

**THE GIN BLOSSOMS, LEFT TO RIGHT: PHILLIP RHODES, SCOTT JOHNSON, BILL LEEN, JESSE VALENZUELA, AND ROBIN WILSON**

Guitarist Jesse Valenzuela of the Gin Blossoms grew up in the Valley, and graduated from Coronado High. The only boy in the family, he has three sisters.

The Gin Blossoms was formed in 1989, and within a year they had released their own indie debut, "Dusted," which caught the ear of A&M Records, who signed the group in 1990. Since then, the Byrds-influenced country/rock-roots group has broken concert records, and sold more than three million CDs in the United States and the United Kingdom. Their 1996 CD, Congratulations I'm Sorry, debuted in the Billboard Top 10. In early 1997, the group was nominated for a Grammy Award.

"We were always making music in the house," says Valenzuela. "We always had a piano, and my father can *sing very well. Success has been a bless-ing for all of us. It changes your whole outlook, for us to be able to stay here, and buy homes on a musician's salary."*

---

*What did you eat, growing up?*

I grew up here and ate what we called neighborhood food: now they call it Southwestern food. Grilled chicken, rice, vegetables, soup. My mom was a good cook, but even then, she didn't want to be held hostage in the kitchen. She didn't cook when she didn't feel like it.

*What do you eat now?*

I live alone and I'm lazy so I don't cook much. But once a week or so, I'll make Spanish rice. Or calabacitas; I'll dice up a squash, add some tomatoes, and cook it in a little olive oil. It's good with French bread. I love to eat red meat but I don't eat much of it. Still, I can eat a rib-eye steak at Ruth's Chris with the best of them.

*What other Valley restaurants do you like?*

For Thai food, I like Malee's on Main Street in Scottsdale. For Mexican food, it's Carolina's; they have great red chile and the best tortillas. Al Cafaro and David Anderle from A&M Records love to go to Los Olivos.

Mr. C's isn't bad, but my favorite Chinese food is Brandy Ho's in San Francisco. I like May West in Tempe, and when I was in high school, the Safari in Scottsdale was a happening place. All these knockout girls hung around there. I think they were call girls, actually.

*Do you like any fast food?*

If I have to, I'll eat a Wendy's hamburger.

*Have any sinful foods you're addicted to?*

Barbecued ribs at Porky's in Memphis, or the Rendezvous, where they have pictures all over of Elvis. The King.

*Are there any foods you hate?*

I don't like jerked chicken. Musicians like to think of themselves as international cats, but I don't like any kind of Caribbean food, or coconut milk.

*What was your peak dining experience?*

It had to be one night in New York City when we were eating with some record executives. It was an Italian place in an old part of the Village, and they just kept bringing the food out. When the band first started, we tried to see how much money we could spend in restaurants. A couple tabs for five or six of us went well over $2,000, but one of the VPs at A&M told us we were barely scratching the surface as compared with some other groups.

---

### SPANISH RICE

2 tablespoons minced onion
1½ cups long-grain white rice
2 tablespoons olive oil
1 teaspoon salt
¼ teaspoon pepper
1 clove fresh garlic, crushed
1 (13¾-ounce) can chicken broth
1 (16-ounce) can whole tomatoes, chopped

*In a large skillet, brown the onion and rice in the oil. Add the remaining ingre-dients. Bring to a boil, cover, and reduce to a simmer for 20 minutes.*
*Serves 4.*

# Tom Weiskopf

At age fifteen, Tom Weiskopf shot ninety-two the first time he played golf. By twenty-six, he had won two major PGA tournaments, and has since taken two dozen more titles, most recently the Pittsburgh Senior Classic in 1996.

Voted Player of the Year in 1973 by fellow professionals and the Golf Writers Association, Weiskopf is also a well-known golf course designer. In Arizona, Weiskopf/Morrish designed Troon, Troon North, and Forest Highlands, all voted by Golf Magazine among the top one hundred courses in the world. The firm also designed the home of the Phoenix Open, the Tournament Players Club.

Weiskopf and his wife, Jeanne, and their two children live in Paradise Valley.

*What did you eat as a child?*

I'm from a German background. My grandparents came over from the old country. So we ate sauerkraut, sausage, dumplings, meat loaf, and noodles. My mom is an excellent cook. Her home-made spaghetti and meatballs were exceptional. And her pastries . . . absolutely great.

*Did you learn to cook?*

The only thing I can do well is over a campfire. I've hunted big game all through the Rocky Mountains, Alaska, the Yukon, Alberta, and I've always enjoyed cooking then. Now I go bird-hunting more. I'll cook quail over the coals.

*Does your wife like to cook?*

Jeanne can cook anything. I have been extremely blessed. Both my mother and mother-in-law are good cooks, and Jeanne is in that category.

*Did you ever have a cooking disaster?*

Sure. One time we were having a party at the house and I brought all these lobster tails to grill. I was getting them ready when the phone rang. While I wasn't pay-ing attention, my bird dog got to them. Out of thirteen lobster tails, only two sur-vived. I don't remember what we ended up serving. Later, it was pretty funny.

*What restaurants do you like?*

Good question. I enjoy When in Naples, Tomaso's, Pizzafarro, Streets of New York, and either one of the Ruth's Chris. I order rib-eye steak, or one of my all-time favorites, steak tartare. I also enjoy the atmosphere at the Downside Risk. There's nothing better than one of their cheese-burgers with a couple of Budweisers.

I enjoy the liquid part of dinner. I love beer, and I'm a red-wine guy. I especially like Silver Oak and Opus wines.

*Addicted to any sinful foods?*

Blueberry pie à la mode is my favorite, with rhubarb pie a close second. I also enjoy carrot cake and chocolate-covered peanuts.

*What was your peak dining experience?*

I've eaten in five-star restaurants around the world, and I've enjoyed those meals, but I don't appreciate them the way some people would. For one thing, I eat so fast. The best meal for me is always around a campfire. You're so cold and tired, any-thing tastes great.

*What should your tombstone say?*

"He should have eaten slower and enjoyed it more."

## JEANNE'S STEAK TARTARE

¾ cup finely minced onion
½ cup (about 1 3½-ounce can) capers, drained
10 anchovy fillets, finely minced
4 egg yolks, lightly beaten
1 teaspoon salt
½ cup finely minced parsley
4 generous shakes Worcestershire sauce
¼ teaspoon fresh, coarsely ground black pepper
2 pounds ground round
Fresh bread, thinly sliced, or water crackers

*In a large bowl, combine all the mari-nade ingredients. Mix with the meat and mound on a large platter, surrounded by the bread or crackers. Serve at room temperature.*
*Serves 8 to 10.*

# Preston Westmoreland

**NANCY AND PRESTON WESTMORELAND**

*KTAR radio talk-show host Preston Westmoreland was born in New Jersey, and remembers as a child being in the peanut gallery once during the live filming of the legendary Howdy Doody show at Rockefeller Center in New York.*

*His earliest ambition was to become a petroleum engineer. "Going out west to look for oil sounded pretty exotic to me," he recalls. Instead, he dropped out of college after two years, and hopped 27,000 miles of rides on freight trains, later entering the marines and going to Vietnam. After the service, he became a newspaper reporter in Beverly Hills, and got a radio job in the 1970s. He moved to Phoenix in 1973 to announce for Dick Van Dyke's KXIV Radio, and*

*joined KTAR five years later. He and his wife, Nancy, have produced two successful outdoor survival videos.*

*The Westmorelands live in Carefree where they can see wildlife from their patio, including deer, javelina, coyotes, and rattlesnakes. "You never go outside without a flashlight in the summertime."*

*What did you eat as a kid?*

We were never gourmets. My parents took me to the Waldorf Astoria for dinner once, but mostly we ate spaghetti, hot dogs, and camp food. We did a lot of camping out.

*What do you like to eat now?*

I'm a real meat-and-potatoes guy. And so is Nancy. We're perfectly matched. Neither of us eats seafood at all. Everybody has a mental thing about something and we're very, very squeamish about fish of any kind.

I like chili, spaghetti, steak, and I'm a real hamburger aficionado. Houston's has the best hamburger in Phoenix. I'm a real sucker for barbecued food, too. Nancy and I can do barbecue better than restaurants. We've found it's more fun to see what you can cook out in the wilderness than in the kitchen at home. We make steak Diane, chicken curry, and tarragon chicken, and Nancy bakes pies. People come over and take pictures of our camp setup.

*Ever have any cooking disasters?*

One time we had some people coming over, and the oven wasn't vented right. I don't know what happened, but the roast burned so much it became this igneous rock. We had to order out for pizza.

Another time we were camping in Death Valley, and this sand blew off the dunes into our hamburgers. There's nothing you can do when sand blows into hamburgers. You can't wash it off.

*What foods do you hate?*

All seafood. We also dislike Oriental food, or any food that's too gourmet-ish.

*What was your peak dining experience?*

We flew to the edge of the Mojave Desert one time and had a big bash with some other friends who flew in. There was nothing around but eight or nine airplanes. Everybody brought something. We had steak, salad, mushrooms, pies. A real feast right at the edge of a dry lake.

*What are your favorite sinful foods?*

I can sit and eat key lime pie, Reese's candy, or pecan pie any time. I love Karsh's [Bakery's] Chinese almond cookies. I have to stay away from Karsh's when I'm watching it.

*What restaurants do you like?*

Morton's, Sfuzzi's, and Cantina del Pedregal. The Palm Court at the Scottsdale Conference Resort is our favorite place to eat. The food is great and it's the best service I've had anywhere in Phoenix.

## BONELESS BARBECUED RIBS

1 (2 to 3-pound) pork loin roast
1 small onion, sliced
2 stalks celery, cut into bite-size chunks
1 (16-ounce) bottle Lea & Perrin's barbecue sauce
2 tablespoons celery seed
1 teaspoon salt
1 tablespoon Lawry's all-purpose seasoning
1 teaspoon jerk seasoning (optional)*
1 to 2 cups water

*Cut the roast into ¾-inch slices. Arrange the slices along the edge of a microwave pressure cooker, alternating with the onion and celery slices.*

*In a large mixing cup, combine ½ cup of the barbecue sauce with all the remaining ingredients. Mix well and pour over the loin slices.*

*Do not fill the pressure-cooker more than three-quarters full! Cook in the microwave 30 to 40 minutes. The pork should be fork-tender when done. Let the pressure cooker cool down about ten minutes (that's part of the cooking time).*

*Remove the loin slices and discard everything else. Put the loin slices on a hot grill and cook until browned and crispy. Just before they are done, brush them with the remaining barbecue sauce.*

*Serves 4 to 6.*

*\*Be careful; it is very hot. The best kind is a thick paste with the brand name Walker's Wood.*

# Paul Westphal

**MICHAEL AND PAUL WESTPHAL**

*Paul Westphal grew up in Redondo Beach, California, and moved to Phoenix to play for the Phoenix Suns in 1975. He became a four-time All-Star and is fifth on the Suns' all-time scoring list with 9,564 points. He was assistant to coach Cotton Fitzsimmons for four years before taking over as coach from 1992 to 1995; his first season as head coach saw the Suns finish with the NBA's best record and the best in club history at 62-20, the first time a Suns team reached the 60-win plateau. He guided the team to its second conference title and a second trip to the NBA finals.*

*Westphal lives in Paradise Valley with his wife, Cindy, and their children, Tori, twenty-one, and Michael, seventeen.*

*How did you learn to cook?*

I don't know that I did. But I can boil water and punch buttons on the microwave.

*What's your favorite sinful food?*

Häagen Dazs chocolate ice cream with fresh raspberries and fragments of See's Victoria Toffee on top. Or Marie Callender's fresh peach pie.

*Your favorite healthful food?*

I don't think there is such a thing when you read that even air can kill you. Too much of anything'll kill you.

*What's your favorite fast food?*

How can you even ask that? Whataburger! It has nothing to do with my contract—they're just great. When people see me eating out and I'm not in a Whataburger, I tell them I'm waiting for them to put one closer to me.

*What was your peak culinary experience?*

It's probably a five-way tie between the fried chicken at Stroud's in Kansas City, the corned beef sandwich at the Carnegie Deli in New York City, the hot turkey dinner at Pepe's in a bowling alley in Los Angeles, a steak at Ruth's Chris, and anything my wife cooks, but I can't remember when the last time that was. I like places that aren't necessarily fancy but that take pride in having good, fresh food.

*What's your most hated food?*

Liver. I didn't like it as a kid, and I've never given it another chance.

*What should your tombstone say?*

"He died with a full stomach." I'm not afraid to die. I see all these old people who get so skinny that they don't have a butt. I want to make sure that I die with a butt.

**PAUL'S BURGER**

*You just grill a regular burger, but you put—and this sounds crazy but—Tony Roma's barbecue sauce, Carnegie Deli mustard, crunchy peanut butter, sliced avocado, hamburger dill pickle slices, and cheddar cheese, on a good bun, like the ones at Fuddrucker's. People laugh, but when I get them to try it, they love it.*

# Grant Woods

MARLENE GALAN ATTEMPTS TO GET THE ATTORNEY GENERAL TO EAT A VEGETABLE.

*Arizona attorney general Grant Woods grew up in Mesa, the son of a developer and a schoolteacher. He moved to Los Angeles in the 1970s to attend Occidental College where he graduated Phi Beta Kappa. He returned to Arizona to attend law school at ASU. Since 1990, he has been the state's top legal eagle, presiding over a staff of 850 which includes 250 attorneys.*

*Woods is married to Marlene Galan, news anchor at KSAZ-Channel 10, and has four children: Austin, fourteen; Lauren, eleven; Cole, six; and Dylan, two.*

*What'd you like to eat as a kid?*

Not much. I was even more picky then than I am now. My mom was a good cook, and we were—are—the type of family that cooks a meal and has dinner together every night. But I couldn't stand vegetables—any vegetable—and I never had a salad until I was probably thirty. I've had maybe two or three apples in my life.

*Did you learn to cook?*

Oh, I could fix my own junk food. Baloney sandwiches on white bread with Miracle Whip. I know, I know, some people are Miracle Whip people and some are mayonnaise people. But I could even eat a Miracle Whip sandwich without meat. I think that's called the Wish Sandwich, you wish you had some meat. One thing I have done is moved away from white to wheat bread.

*Any foods you hate now?*

Most vegetables, liver, kidneys . . . look, what it really comes down to, it's easier to tell you what I do like: hamburgers, hot dogs, Mexican food, Italian food, and Cuban food. Marlene's Cuban, and we eat Cuban a lot. Rice, chicken. I'm very frustrating to her; I'm like the fourth child. Before I can leave the table, I have to eat one carrot, one piece of broccoli . . .

*Have any favorite dining memories?*

All the time. I can be anywhere in the world and be not just satisfied but thrilled: There's always a Whataburger or a McDonald's. I don't need the five-star restaurants. When I was going to school in L.A., I ate cheeseburgers every day at Pete's Fish and Chips, this little Greek place. Two years later, I went back there and Pete's wife saw me, and said, "Look, look, it's Mayonnaise-and-Cheese-Only." They all came running out to see me.

*But any all-time peak experiences, food-wise?*

Sure. The night before the election, I had a six-pack of tacos and a bean burro from Taco Bell, a Big Mac, and a slice of Domino's Pizza, all in one sitting.

*What other restaurants do you like?*

Guedo's Taco Shop in Chandler, and Vincent's. For all the awards Vincent has won, the fact that he ranks right up there with Guedo's says it all for me.

*Do you eat any healthful food?*

Oatmeal. In restaurants. I don't have lunch; any meetings I have over a meal are breakfast because I try to play basketball at lunch.

*Your wife says your eating habits are "pathetic." What say you?*

I've only been sick three days in my adult life. I think the secret is preservatives. Heavy on the Hostess Twinkies. Either I'm going to keel over any minute or I'm going to live to 120, and I'll be very well preserved.

## MARLENE'S CHICHARITAS

*"This is kind of tedious but it's really easy. They're great with yellow rice and chicken as a side dish, or as an appetizer. In Cuba, they're the equivalent of chips in a Mexican restaurant."*

Five plantain bananas, peeled and
    sliced very thin
1 cup canola oil
Salt to taste

*Heat the oil in a medium frying pan. Drop the plantain slices into the oil one by one, flipping them until they get brown and crunchy. Remove, drain on paper towels, and sprinkle with salt.*
   *Serves 6.*

# Index

Actors
  Miller, Ann, 94–95
  Mitchum, Jim, 96–97
  Perrine, Valerie, 106–107
Adrian's Mexican Food, 93
Agusti's, 49
Air France, 92
AJ's, 98
AJ's Barbecue, 59
Ajo Al's, 61
Al's Friend Sharon's
  Caesar-at-His-Finest Salad, 45
"Al's World," 44
Albondigas, 57
Alice Cooper Celebrity Golf
  Tournament, 26
Allegro's, 85
Allen, Steve, 116
Allende, Isabel, 21
America West Arena, 22
American Express, 36
Ammaccapane, Danielle, 2–3
Ammaccapane, Ralph (elder), 2, 37
Ammaccapane, Ralph (younger), 2, 3
Ammaccapane's Linguine with Clam
  Sauce, 3
Ammaccapane's Restaurant and
  Sports Bar, 2
Anchovies, 69
Anderle, David, 129
Andres, Bill, 1, 4–5
Angeli, Pier, 32
Anne Coe's Unexpected-Company
  Black Bean Cakes, 21
Anthony's, 49
Apollo Theatre, 58–59
Apple Pancakes, 103
Arbonne International, 36
Arby's Horsey Sauce, 5
Arcadia Farms, 13
Arcadia High, 124
Arizona, University of, 72, 102, 106

Arizona Biltmore, 24, 26, 60
Arizona Biltmore Cheesecake, 25
Arizona Board of Regents, 8
Arizona Children's Burn Camp, 4
Arizona Diamondbacks, 22
Arizona Grill, 79, 97
*Arizona Highways*, 127
Arizona Humane Society, 60
*The Arizona Republic*, 1, 70, 86, 110
Arizona Save-A-Life Alliance, 98
Arizona State University, 10, 28, 46,
  52, 62, 66, 80, 136
Arizona Women in Radio &
  Television, 60
Arizonans for Cultural
  Development, 12
Arpaio, Ava, 6
Arpaio, Joe, 1, 6–7
Arpaio, Rocco, 6
Arpaio, Sherry, 6
Art Center College, 92
Arthur Godfrey Talent Show, 88
Artists
  Coe, Anne, 20–21
  Gorman, R. C., 54–55
  Guerrero, Zarco, 56–57
  Keane, Bil, 10, 70–71
  Mahaffey, Merrill, 80–81
  McCall, Robert, 82–83
  Mell, Ed, 92–93
  Scholder, Fritz, 114–115
  Shields, Robert, 118–119
*The Artists and Writers Cookbook*, 115
Asimov, Isaac, 82
AT&T, 36
Athletes. *See* Sports figures
Aubergine, 125
Austin, Bill, 86
Avanti's, 9, 11, 31, 35, 39, 41, 49, 85,
  97, 107
Ayako, 27
AZ 88, 115

Babci's Lobster Thermidor, 63
Baby Kay's, 13, 53
Bailey, Eileen, 1
Baker's Square, 59
Bamboo Club, 61
Bank One Ballpark, 22
Barbecued Ribs, 133
Barrett, Barbara, 92
Barrett, Craig, 92
Barry Goldwater Jr.'s Chicken-in-a-
  Bag, 53
Baruch College, 76
Basha, Eddie, 8–9
Bashas' supermarkets, 8, 37, 98
  ice cream, 9
Baskin Robbins, 59
*The Beat Generation*, 97
Beef Eaters, 99
Beef Stew, 83
Begin, Menachem, 53
Bell, Bob Boze, 93
Ben & Jerry's Chunky Monkey ice
  cream, 48
*The Best Salad*, 121
*Beyond the Visible Terrain: The Art of Ed
  Mell*, 92
The Big Apple, 31
Big Pete Pearson & the Blues
  Sevilles, 104
Big Pete's Peach Cobbler, 105
Bill's Campfire Halibut, 5
Bistro Vagara, 31
Black Bean Cakes, 21
Black Bean Salad, 87
The Black Rose, 87
Blake, Brennan, 86
Blake, Bridget, 86
Blake, Lee, 86
Blake, Shannon, 86
Blinis, 89
Blue Burrito, 53
Blueberry pie, 131

Blues Blast, 111
Bobbi's Apple Pancakes, 103
Bobby McGee's, 69
Bocuse, Paul, 27
Bombeck, Andy, 10–11
Bombeck, Betsy, 10–11
Bombeck, Bill, 10–11, 92
Bombeck, Erma, 10–11, 92
Bombeck, Eva Louise, 10
Bombeck, Jackie, 10
Bombeck, Matt, 10–11
Boneless Barbecued Ribs, 133
Boston College, 62
Boston Market, 35, 87, 103
Brandy Ho's, 129
Brezhnev, Leonid, 119
Brigham Young University, 34
Broadcasters
  Andres, Bill, 1, 4–5
  Cavazos, Carol, 1, 18–19
  Damone, Perry, 32–33
  Dana, Kent, 34–35
  Davenport, Rita, 36–37
  Downs, Hugh, 38–39
  Feinberg, Al, 44–45
  Garagiola, Joe, 48–49
  Heywood, Bill, 60–61
  Hitchcock, Tara, 62–63
  Liddy, G. Gordon, 1, 74–75
  McDonald, Beth, 86–87
  McMahon, Pat, 90–91
  Pratt, Dave, 108–109
  Steiger, Sam, 122–123
  Westmoreland, Preston, 132–133
Broccoli Pasta, 89
Brodeto, 117
Brokaw, Tom, 83
*Brother, Brother, Stop*, 120
Brown, Benjamin, 76
Brown, James, 58
Brussels sprouts, 49
Bua, Cathy, 13

Buchanan, Bryce, 40
Buchanan, Jamie Drinkwater, 40
Buchanan, Kelsie, 40
Burger King, 39
Businesspeople
    Basha, Eddie, 8–9
    Colangelo, Jerry, 22–23
    Earnhardt, Tex, 42–43
    Goldwater, Barry Jr., 52–53
    Hormel, Geordie, 53, 64–65
    Mackay, Harvey, 78–79
Butternut Squash Soup, 65
"By the Time I Get to Phoenix," 14

Cadbury chocolate, 45
Caen, Herb, 118
Caesar salad, 33, 45
Cafaro, Al, 129
Cafera Piñot Noir, 119
Calf brains, 81
Camelback High, 106
Camelback Inn, 75
Campana, Cassidy, 12
Campana, Katie, 12
Campana, Richard, 12
Campana, Richie, 12
Campana, Sam Kathryn, 12–13
Campbell, Ashley, 14
Campbell, Cal, 14
Campbell, Glen, 1, 14–15
Campbell, Kim, 14
Campbell, Shanon, 14
Cancun Jazz Festival, 120
Cannes Film Festival, 106
Cantina del Pedregal, 133
Carbajal, Daniella, 16
Carbajal, Danny, 16
Carbajal, Erica, 16
Carbajal, Merci, 16
Carbajal, Micaela, 16
Carbajal, Michael, 16–17
Carbajal, Michelangelo, 16
Carbajal, Mikito, 16
Carlos O'Brien's, 99
Carl's Meats, 13
Carnegie Deli, 135
Carolina's, 129
Carrot cake, 41
Carson, Johnny, 116
Carter, Jimmy, 74
Casa Cordova, 55
Casa de Los Niños, 98

Cavazos, Carol, 1, 18–19
Caviar, 127
Center Against Sexual Assault, 21
Chandler School Board, 8
Channel 10, 34
Channel 15, 44
Charles, Ray, 14
Chasen's, 11
Cheesecake, 17, 25
    recipe, 25
Cheney, Brian, 53
Cherry, Jim, 93
Cherry Surprise, 11
Chianti, 47, 125
Chicago Bulls, 22
Chicano Convict Guacamole, 75
Chicharitas, 137
Chicken
    Barry Goldwater Jr.'s Chicken-in-
        a-Bag, 53
    Chicken Salad, 27
    Francine's Fabulous Fried
        Chicken, 111
    Rita's Chicken Enchiladas, 37
Childsplay, 56
Chile Connection, 55
Chili (chile)
    Chili for 200, 79
    Glen Campbell's Favorite Chili, 15
    Jackie Drinkwater's Chili Verde, 41
    Lattie's Chile Paste, 29
    Marshall Trimble's Cowboy Chili,
        127
    Rose's Red Chile, 55
    Tex-Mex Chili, 95
China Doll, 9
Chinois, 115
Chitlins, 37
Chocolate Cake, 93
Christo's, 67, 85, 99
Christopher's, 23, 61, 63, 65, 95, 109
Christopher's Bistro, 51, 85
CIA, 76
City University of New York, 76
Claiborne, Craig, 51
Clam Sauce and Linguine, 3
Clark, Mary Higgins, 31
Clive's Guava-Prawn Sauté, 31
Coe, Anne, 20–21
Colangelo, Jerry, 22–23
Colangelo, Joan, 22
Cole, Ike, 24–25

Cole, Margie, 25
Cole, Nat King, 14, 24, 25
Coleman's dry mustard, 33
Collins, Phil, 100
Colorado River Dinner, 81
Colter, Jessi, 68
Congratulations I'm Sorry, 128
Contreras, Waldo, 93
Cooking With Rita, 36
Cool Whip, 11
Cooper, Alice, 26, 27
Cooper, Calico, 26
Cooper, Dash, 26
Cooper, Sheryl, 26–27
Cooper, Sonora, 26
Coor, Elva, 28
Coor, Lattie, 28–29
Coosa and Sautéed Zucchini, 9
Cordon Bleu, 95
Corn Bread, 69
Corn-Bread Stuffing, 101
Corn Chowder, 71
Coronado High, 128
Coyote Springs Brewing, 5
Crazy Jim's, 51
Creamed corn, 87
Cunetto's, 49
Cussler, Barbara, 30
Cussler, Clive, 1, 30–31

Da Vang, 17
Damone, Perry, 32–33
Damone, Vic, 32
Dana, Janet, 34
Dana, Kent, 1, 34–35
Dancers
    Cooper, Sheryl, 26–27
    Miller, Ann, 94–95
Darrah, Marlin, 114
Davenport, David, 36
Davenport, Michael, 36
Davenport, Rita, 36–37, 127
Davenport, Scott, 36
Davis, Dan, 63
De Grazia and Mexican Cookery, 36
Dean, John, 74
Denny's, 109
Desert Inn, 106
DeVito, Danny, 54
Diamond, Neil, 68
Different Pointe of View, 63
Dig Your Well Before You're Thirsty, 78

Dinty Moore Beef Stew, 65
Dinty Moore Products, 64
Divinity, 99
Dixon, Maynard, 92
Doc's Pasta Chi Chi, 117
Doll and DeLuca, 95
Dominic's, 49
Domino's Pizza, 137
Don & Charlie's, 13, 15, 47
Dooley, Virginia, 55
Dora's Ham Loaf, 35
Dorothy McGuire's Broccoli Pasta, 89
Doubletree Inn, 93
Downs, Deirdre, 38
Downs, Hugh, 38–39
Downs, Hugh Jr., 38
Downs, Ruth, 38
Downside Risk, 131
Drinkwater, Herb, 40–41
Drinkwater, Jackie, 40, 41
Drinkwater, Jamie, 40
Drinkwater's, 41, 71
Drug Enforcement Administration,
    6, 74
Duck 'n Decanter, 61
Duck Soup, 119
Duke Wayne's Tamale Pie, 97
Duncan, Sandy, 54
Duran, Roberto, 16
Durant's, 85, 93, 109
"Dusted," 128
Dyke & the Blazers, 58

E. F. Hutton, 106
Earnhardt, Hal, 42
Earnhardt, Jim Babe, 42
Earnhardt, Pam, 42
Earnhardt, Tex, 42–43
Eating, 1
Ed Debevic's, 5
Eddie's Grill, 27, 61, 87, 93
Educators
    Coor, Lattie, 28–29
    Lovett, Clara, 76–77
Eel, 47
The Eggery, 59
8700, 41
El Bravo, 67, 99, 117
El Chorro, 11, 71, 75
El Saguarito, 103
El Tovar, 67, 127
Elaine's, 107

Eliana's, 93
Elks Club, 58
Enchiladas, 37
Erma's Mom's Strawberry Delight, 11
Escargot. *See* Snails
*Esquire,* 92
Ethiopian food, 113
Explorers Club, 31

*Family Circus,* 70
Famous Amos, 37
The Farm, 21
Father of the Year, 102
Father's Day Council, 102
FBI, 74
Febergé, 92
Feinberg, Al, 44–45
Fierros, Norman, 51
Filiberto's, 5
Fish, 71
Fish Market, 117
Fisher, M. F. K., 1
Fitzsimmons, Cotton, 47, 134
5 & Diner, 59
Flank Steak, 51
Fleetwood Mac, 64
Fleming, Paul, 73
Food, 1
Forbes, Dorita, 41
Ford, Jineane, 34
Ford Foundation, 114
Forest Highlands, 130
Fortune Cookie, 105
Foundation for Burns and Trauma, 4
Four Courts, 105
Francine's Fabulous Fried Chicken,
    111
Franco's Trattoria, 41
Frango Mint Cookies, 13
Frankie's, 71
Franklin, Aretha, 58
Fried Chicken, 111
Frieder, Bill, 46–47
Frieder, Janice, 46–47
Frieder, Laura, 46, 47
Fuddruckers, 97

Galan, Marlene, 136
Garagiola, Audrie, 48
Garagiola, Gina, 48, 49
Garagiola, Joe, 1, 48–49
Garagiola, Joe Jr., 48, 49

Garagiola, Steve, 48, 49
Garcia's, 15
Gardiner's Tennis Ranch, 78
Gazpacho, 11
    Gazpacho from Barcelona, 115
Geha's Restaurant, 87
Gelato, 117
*Genghis Khan,* 97
"Gentle on My Mind," 14
George Mason University, 76
George Washington University, 76
Gerard, Michel, 27
Gert's Chocolate Cake, 93
Ghirardelli chocolate, 119
Giese, John, 4
Gill-Rimsza, Kim, 112
Gin Blossoms, 128
Girardet's, 91
Glen Campbell's Favorite Chili, 15
Goddard, Judy, 50
Goddard, Sam, 50
Goddard, Terry, 50–51
Godiva chocolate, 119
Golden Rule Cafe, 59
Golden Swan, 41
Goldwater, Barry Jr., 1, 52–53
Goldwater, Barry Sr., 52–53
*Golf Magazine,* 130
Golf Writers Association, 130
Gonzales, Andy, 111
Gonzales, Carmen, 111
Goo-Goo Bars, 37
The Good Egg, 59, 75
Good Morning Arizona, 62
Gordon, Shep, 27
Gorman, Carl, 55
Gorman, R. C., 54–55
Governor's Arts Award, 56
Grandma's Outrageous Fantasy Pie, 61
*The Grass Is Always Greener over the
    Septic Tank,* 10
Greekfest, 87
Green Potatoes, 47
The Grill at the Ritz Carlton, 39
Grodin, Charles, 83
Gross, Chris, 109
Ground beef, 9
Guacamole, 19, 75
Guava-Prawn Sauté, 31
Guedo's Taco Shop, 57, 109, 137
Guerithault, Vincent, 115
Guerrero, Carmen, 57

Guerrero, Quentzal, 57
Guerrero, Tizoc, 57
Guerrero, Zarco, 56–57
Guerrero, Zarina, 57
*Guideposts,* 48

Häagen Dazs ice cream, 107, 135
The Hacienda, 83
Hagerty, Donald J., 92
Halibut, 5
Ham Loaf, 35
Hamilton, Jean, 59
Hamilton, Nancy Cordelia, 59
Hamilton, Paul, 58–59
Hamilton, Shirley, 59
Harkins, Danny, 13
Harvard University, 50, 54
Havana Cafe, 13, 31, 93
Hayes, Isaac, 100
Healthy Choice, 19
Henley, Don, 100
*Here's the Southwestern Desert,* 20
Hermitage Museum, 114
Hershey chocolate, 45
Hershey's Kisses, 13
Heston, Charlton, 97
Hewitt, Don, 79
Heywood, Bill, 60–61
Hilton, Conrad, 94
Hitchcock, Tara, 62–63
Holly, Buddy, 68, 69
Honeybears Barbecue, 109
Honeywell, 36
Hopi Elementary School, 26
Hops, 61
Hormel, Geordie, 53, 64–65
Hormel, Geri, 64
Hormel, Gillian, 64
Hormel, Jamie, 64
Hormel Company, 64
Hormel's Onion Soup, 65
Horny Toad, 39
Horvath, Robert "Bronco," 20
Hostess Twinkies, 137
Houston, University of, 18
Houston's, 43, 61, 63, 87, 127, 133
Hughes, Howard, 94
Hull, Jane Dee, 66–67
Hull, Terrance, 66
Humorists
    Trimble, Marshall, 126–127
Hyatt Gainey Ranch, 41, 63

Iacocca, Lee, 89
Ianuzzi, 39
Ichiban Records, 111
International Boxing Federation, 16
International Film and Video, 114
Irvin, Kevin, 93
Italian American Club, 117

J. Chew's, 25
Jack in the Box, 17, 49
Jackie Drinkwater's Chili Verde, 41
Jacquelina's, 55
Jalapeños, 41
Japan Fellowship, 56
Javelina, 113
JD pie, 67
JD's, 68
Jeanne's Steak Tartare, 131
Jell-O, 11, *77*
Jennings, Shooter, 68, 69
Jennings, Waylon, 1, 68–69, 126
Jerry's Deli, 53
Jiffy Pop, 109
Joe's Father's Tomato Sauce, 7
Joey's, 95
John Hancock Building, 19
Johnny Rocket's, 23
Johnson, Scott, 128
Jordan's, 35
Joseph's Table, 55
Joy Tash Gallery, 20
Joyce's Corn-Bread Stuffing, 101
Judy's, 95
*Just Wait till You Have Children of Your
    Own!,* 10

Kansas, University of, 66, 76
KBMT, 62
KCOH, 32
KDKB, 4
Keane, Bil, 10, 70–71
Keane, Christopher, 70
Keane, Gayle, 70
Keane, Glen, 70
Keane, Jeff, 70
Keane, Neal, 70
Keane, Thelma, 70, 71
Keegan's, 47
Kennedy Center, 56
Kesling, Rod, 2, 3
KEZ, 32, 33, 86
KFC, 115

KHJ, 32
Kidneys, 71, 89, 137
*Kill the Lawyers*, 123
King, Larry, 83
King, Stephen, 31
Kiwi, 61
Kleber, John, 93
Kool-Aid, 59
KPHO, 90
KPNX, 34
Kristler Chardonnay, 119
KSAZ, 136
KTAR, 86, 90, 91, 132
KTVK, 62
Kunz, Edith, 69
KUPD, 108
KUSK, 122
KXIV, 132
Kyl, Caryll, 72, 73
Kyl, John, 72
Kyl, Jon, 72–73
Kyl, Kristi, 72
Kyoto, 109

La Casa Vieja, 99
La Fontanella, 33
La Locanda, 19
La Parrilla Suiza, 115
La Rendezvous, 103, 129
Ladies' Professional Golf
    Association, 2
Lamb, 9
Lambert's, 55
Latilla at the Boulders, 41
Lattie Coor Elementary School, 28
Lattie's Chile Paste, 29
L'Auberge, 95
Law enforcement officials
    Arpaio, Joe, 1, 6–7
Le Peep's, 75
Leachman, Cloris, 54
Lean Cuisine, 19, 67
Lee, Monica, 50, 51
Leen, Bill, 128
Leland's, 41
Lemon Bars, 113
Leon, Jon, 119
Lewis, Jerry Lee, 126
Library of Congress, 76
Liddy, G. Gordon, 1, 74–75
Linguine with Clam Sauce, 3
Linlahr, Victor H., 71

Liver, 1, 10, 19, 21, 25, 31, 45, 71, 89,
    125, 135, 137
Livi, Angelo, 97, 107
Livi, Patsy, 107
Lobster Thermidor, 63
Los Compadres, 35
Los Dos Molinos, 29, 57, 91, 97
Los Olivos, 49, 115, 129
Louie's on the Lake, 19
Louise's Beef Stew, 83
Lovett, Clara, 76–77
Lovett, Lyle, 110
Low-Fat Corn Bread, 69
Luke's, 19
Lutefisk, 103, 115

M&Ms, 5, 27, 67, 125
Macayo's, 35, 49, 107
Mackay Envelope, 78
Mackay, Carol Ann, 78, 79
Mackay, Harvey, 78–79
Mahaffey, Jeanne, 80
Mahaffey, Merrill, 80–81
Maid-Rites, 85
*Making Time, Making Money*, 36
Malee's, 129
*Mame*, 94
Mancuso's, 49, 95
Mandarin Delight, 67
Marceau, Marcel, 119
Marcella's, 9
Marche Gourmet, 61
Marco Polo, 13, 87
Maria's, 53
Maria's When in Naples, 41, 87,
    97, 131
Maricopa County sheriff, 6–7
Marie Callender's, 61, 135
Marlene's Chicharitas, 137
Marshall Trimble's Cowboy Chili, 127
Martini Ray Cabernet Sauvignon, 119
Marx, Groucho, 119
Mary Kitchen Roast Beef Hash, 65
Maryland Inn, 113
*La Mascarada*, 56
Massachusetts, University of—
    Amherst, 44
May West, 129
McCall, Louise, 82
McCall, Robert, 1, 82–83
McCoy, Al, 84–85
McCoy, Georgia, 84, 85

McCoy's Favorite Shish Kebab, 85
McDonald, Beth, 86–87
McDonald's, 15, 19, 49, 115, 123, 137
McDuffey's, 47
McGuire, Dorothy. *See* Williamson,
    Dorothy McGuire
McGuire Sisters, 88
McMahon, Adelaide, 90
McMahon, Duffy, 90, 91
McMahon, Jack, 90
McMahon, Pat, 90–91, 126
McRae, Joyce, 100, 101
Meat Loaf, 123
Mecham, Evan, 98
Mell, Carter, 92
Mell, Ed, 92–93
Mell, Taylor, 92
Melton, Bob, 108
Menudo, 8
Merci's Tortillas, 17
Mesa Southwest Museum, 80
Metropolitan Museum of Art, 54, 80
Mi Patio, 51
Michigan University, 46
Middle Eastern Bakery, 93
Middle Tennessee State University, 36
Mikado, 93
Milano's, 85
Miller, Ann, 94–95
Mirabelle, 89
Miracle Mile, 93
Miracle Whip, 137
Miss Karen's yogurt, 103
Miss Porter's School, 124
Mitchum, Caitlin, 96
Mitchum, Dorothy, 96
Mitchum, Jim, 96–97
Mitchum, Price, 96
Mitchum, Robert, 96
Mitchum, Spence, 96
Mofford, Rose, 1, 98–99
Mom's Pizzelles, 23
Mom's Veggie Dressing, 121
Momaday, N. Scott, 114
The Monastery, 63
Monti's, 47
Moon Garden, 43
Moore, Sam, 100–101
Morton's, 53, 73, 133
Morton's Steakhouse, 9
Mr. C's, 95, 129
Mrs. White's Golden Rule Cafe, 117

Mulligan's, 41
Mullins, Michael, 95
Musicians
    Campbell, Glen, 1, 14–15
    Cole, Ike, 24–25
    Guerrero, Zarco, 56–57
    Hamilton, Paul, 58–59
    Jennings, Waylon, 1, 68–69
    Moore, Sam, 100–101
    Pearson, Pete, 104–105
    Reed, Francine, 110–111
    Severinsen, Doc, 116–117
    Sledge, Debbie, 120–121
    Valenzuela, Jesse, 128–129
    Williamson, Dorothy McGuire,
        88–89
Myers, Pat, 110

Nantucket Lobster Trap, 59
National Aeronautics and Space
    Administration, 82
National Air and Space Museum, 82
National Cartoonists Society, 70
National Endowment for the Arts, 56
*National Lampoon*, 92
National Security Council, 36
Navajo Codetalkers, 55
Navajo Gallery, 54
Navajo Reservation, 54
NBC, 38, 39, 48
Nello's Pizza, 47
Nestle's Crunch, 45
*New York Times*, 51
The News Cafe, 125
Nieporent, Drew, 21
Nixon, Richard, 74, 124
North High School, 40, 92
Northern Arizona University, 54, 76
Northwestern University, 62
Notre Dame, 83
*Nudes & Foods*, 55

Oatmeal, 43
Oaxaca, 97, 111
Occidental College, 136
Octopus, 47
O'Keeffe, Georgia, 92
Olive Garden, 17, 83
Olives, 111
Olson, Bobbi, 102
Olson, Lute, 102–103

Olson, Scott, 16
Onassis, Jacqueline, 54
Orpheum Theatre, 94
The Other Place, 13, 31
The Outback, 85
Oysters, 83, 91

P. F. Chang's, 5, 15, 17, 23, 27, 35, 71,
    87, 115
Paar, Jack, 38
Pacino, Al, 54
*Painting the Paradox*, 114
The Palm, 103
Palm Court, 41, 133
Palm Springs Desert Art Museum, 80
Pancakes, 103
Parsnips, 117
Pasta
    Doc's Pasta Chi Chi, 117
    Dorothy McGuire's Broccoli
        Pasta, 89
    Pasta Shields, 119
    Shrimp Pasta Salad, 91
    Valerie's Pasta Thing, 107
Pasta sauces
    Ammaccapane's Linguine with
        Clam Sauce, 3
    Joe's Father's Tomato Sauce, 7
    Salsa di Nina Piero, 33
Paula Pratt's Pretzels and Beer, 109
Paul's Burger, 135
PBS, 56
Peach Cobbler, 105
Peanut butter, 31
Pearson, Barbara, 105
Pearson, Pete, 104–105
Pecan pie, 85
Pepe's, 135
PepsiCo, 36
Perrine, Ken, 106
Perrine, Renee, 106
Perrine, Valerie, 106–107
Perry, Paul, 114
Pete's Fish and Chips, 137
The Phoenician, 31, 65, 83, 95
Phoenix, Arizona, 2
Phoenix Art Museum, 92
Phoenix Board of Realtors, 112
*Phoenix Business Journal*, 51
Phoenix College, 40, 80, 92
Phoenix Coyotes, 22
Phoenix Giants, 84

Phoenix Open, 40, 130
Phoenix Suns, 22, 84, 134
Phoenix Symphony, 116
Pickett, Wilson, 58
Pietro's, 119
Pigs' ears, 111
Pigs' feet, 103, 111
Piñata, 23
Pink Pony, 85
Piñon Grill, 31
Pischke's, 53, 97
Pittsburgh Senior Classic, 130
Pizza Hut, 115
Pizzafaro, 131
Pizzelles, 23
Pizzeria Bianco, 23, 93
Pizzeria Uno, 85
The Pleasures of the Palette, 21
Pointe Hilton, 69
Politicians
    Arpaio, Joe, 1, 6–7
    Campana, Sam Kathryn, 12–13
    Drinkwater, Herb, 40–41
    Goddard, Terry, 50–51
    Goldwater, Barry Jr., 52–53
    Hull, Jane Dee, 66–67
    Kyl, Jon, 72–73
    Mofford, Rose, 98–99
    Rimsza, Skip, 112–113
    Steiger, Sam, 122–123
    Symington, Ann (Arizona's first
        lady), 124–125
    Woods, Grant, 136–137
Pork Roast, 73
Porky's, 129
Portofino, 85
Prater, David, 100
Pratt, Dave, 108–109
Pratt, David Jr., 108
Pratt, Kyle, 108
Pratt, Lorne, 108
Pratt, Paula, 108
Prawns, 31
Pretzels, 109
Primitive Baptist Church, 100
Pritzlaff, John, Jr., 124
Prosciutto, 33
Pugzie's, 61
Purple Heart, 122

Quickest Wit Award, 86
The Quilted Bear, 75

Rabbit Cacciatore, 77
Raffaele's Arbor, 2
*Raise the Titanic!*, 30
"Ramblin' Rose," 24
Rancho Mañana, 39
Rancho Pinot Grill, 13, 79, 93
Raveling, George, 46
Rawhide, 105
Red Chile, 55
The Red Sea, 113
Redding, Otis, 58
Reed, Francine, 1, 110–111
Reed, Margo, 110
Renee's, 95
The Renegade, 55
Reuben award, 70
The Rex, 87
*Rhinestone Cowboy*, 14
Rhodes, Phillip, 128
Rhubarb pie, 131
Rhythm Room, 111
The Rib Hut, 45
Ricardo's, 111
Richardson, Bill, 54
Richardson's, 97
Richmond College, 32
Rimsza, Alexander, 112
Rimsza, Brian, 112
Rimsza, Jenny, 112
Rimsza, Nicole, 112
Rimsza, Skip, 112–113
Rimsza, Taylor, 112
Risotto alla Milanese, 49
Rita's Chicken Enchiladas, 37
Ritz Carlton, 125
Robinson, Bill Bojangles, 94
Rock & Roll Hall of Fame, 100
Rock Springs, 67, 97
Rockefeller, Winthrop, 15
Rockefeller Foundation, 114
Rogers, Will, 48
Rooney, Mickey, 94
Rosario's, 85
Rose's Divinity, 99
Rose's Red Chile, 55
Rose's Salsa, 98
Rousseline Hotel, 27
"Route 66," 24
RoxSand's, 21, 31, 71
Roybal, Rose, 54
Ruth's Chris, 23, 69, 129, 131, 135

Saba, Marian, 13
Sadat, Anwar, 53
Safari, 129
Saguaro Cafe, 41
Sakura, 103
Salad, 121
Salsa di Nina Piero, 33
Salute, 67, 97
Sam & Dave, 58, 100
Sam's Cafe, 5, 63
Sam's Frango Mint Cookies, 13
San Carlos Bay, 17
San Francisco State University, 124
Sandale, 63
Sarde, Cliff, 93
Satisfied Frog, 35, 39
Savarin, Brillat, 1
*Scandals of 1939*, 94
Scholder, Fritz, 114–115
Schwarzenegger, Arnold, 54, 92
Scottsdale Arts Council Chairman's
    Artist Award, 56
Scottsdale Center for the Arts, 93
Scottsdale Community College, 126
Scottsdale Farmer's Market, 13
Scottsdale Princess, 65
Scratch 'N Sniff Awards, 60
Scripps College, 124
Sea urchins, 33
Seafood, 133
See's candy, 95, 135
*Seinfeld*, 83
Serrano's Mexican Food, 9
Severinsen, Doc, 116–117
Severinsen, Emily, 116, 117
Sfuzzi, 5, 133
Shamrock, 9
Shells at Mountain Shadows, 71
Shields, Rhonda, 118
Shields, Robert, 118–119
Shields & Yarnell, 118
Shish Kebab, 85
Shivel, Phillip, 119
Shrimp Pasta Salad, 91
Shrimp Sausage Hors D'Oeuvres, 67
Shughrue's Hillside, 95
Sikora, Bob, 69
Silver Star, 122
Sinatra, Frank, 14, 119
Singers. *See* Musicians

Sister Sledge, 120
*60 Minutes,* 79
Skip's Favorite Lemon Bars, 113
Sledge, Carol, 120
Sledge, Debbie, 120–121
Sledge, Joni, 120, 121
Sledge, Kathy, 120
Sledge, Kim, 120
Small Paul & Drivin' Wheel, 58
Small Paul's Tacos, 59
Smithsonian Institution, 80
Snails, 11, 47, 79, 95
Snickers Bars, 63, 79
Solid Rock Foundation, 26
"Soul Man," 100
Southwestern Black Bean Salad, 87
Southwestern Pork Roast, 73
Spam, 55, 61, 65
Spanish Rice, 129
Sports figures
    Ammaccapane, Danielle, 2–3
    Carbajal, Michael, 16–17
    Colangelo, Jerry, 22–23
    Frieder, Bill, 46–47
    McCoy, Al, 84–85
    Olson, Lute, 102–103
    Weiskopf, Tom, 130–131
    Westphal, Paul, 134–135
Springsteen, Bruce, 101
St. Louis Cardinals, 48
St. Vincent de Paul, 98
*Star Trek,* 82
Starworld, 6
State Board of Education, 8
Steak & Sticks, 95
Steak Tartare, 131
Steamers, 31, 49, 69
Steele, Carol, 1
Steely Dan, 64
Steiger, Sam, 122–123
"Stop the World and Let Me Off," 68
Strawberry Delight, 11
Strawberry sauce, 25
Streets of New York, 35, 131
Stroud's, 135
The Studio, 115
Stuffed Zucchini, 39
*Success Strategies,* 36
Such Is Life, 51, 97
*Sugar Babies,* 94
Susan's Righteous Texas Turkey
    Meat Loaf, 61

Sushi, 35, 49, 69
Suzanne Brown Gallery, 80
Swedish Green Potatoes, 47
*Swim With the Sharks Without Being
    Eaten Alive,* 78
Symington, Ann, 124–125
Symington, Fife, 124

Tabasco, 29
Taco Bell, 5, 7, 43, 61, 137
   hot sauce, 5
Tacos
    Small Paul's Tacos, 59
    Tacos de Juarez, 17
Tamale Pie, 97
Tang, 92
Tarbell's, 27, 39, 51, 63, 125
Taylor, Elizabeth, 54
TCBY yogurt, 79
Tee Pee, 5, 11, 23, 115
Teich, Bill, 41
Teich, Georgia, 41
Terrail, Claude, 95
Terry Goddard's Grilled Flank
    Steak, 51
Texas, University of, Austin, 76
TexAz Grill, 99, 123
Tex-Mex Chili, 95
Tex's Morning Oatmeal, 43
Thai Rama, 17
Thel's Queensland Corn Chowder, 71
Three Stooges, 94
*Thunder Road,* 96
Thursday Art Walk, 13
Tico Taco, 93
*Today* show, 38, 48
Tomaso's, 15, 23, 83, 85, 125, 131
Tomato juice, 5
Tomato sauce, 3, 7
*The Tonight Show,* 38, 116
Tornament Players Club, 130
Tortillas, 17
Tours D'Argent, 83, 95
*Track Down,* 97
Trader Joe's, 45
The Trading Post, 55
Tribeca Grill, 21
Trieste, University of, 76
Trimble, Gena, 126
Trimble, Marshall, 1, 126–127
Trimble, Roger, 126
Troon, 130

Troon North, 130
Trout, 81
Truffles, 115
Tuccheti, 13
Turkey Meat Loaf, 61
Turnips, 117
Tutto, 13
*20/20,* 38
*2001: A Space Odyssey,* 82

Unbacio, 41
Uncle Sam's, 87
*Unforgettable,* 24–25
Usry, Kent, 93
U.S. Supreme Court, 80

Vagara Bistro, 115
Valenzuela, Jesse, 128–129
Valerie's Pasta Thing, 107
Valle Luna, 35
Vegetables, 137
Veggie Dressing, 121
Villa Fontana, 55
Vincent's, 9, 11, 31, 39, 41, 51, 67, 79,
    83, 87, 91, 95, 115, 137
   chocolate soufflé, 125
   crème brûlée, 67, 73, 89
   duck tamales, 67, 73

*The Wallace & Ladmo Show,* 90
Walters, Barbara, 39
Warwick, Ruth, 54
*Waylon,* 68
Waylon's Low-Fat Corn Bread, 69
"We Are Family," 120
Weiskopf, Jeanne, 130
Weiskopf, Tom, 130–131
Wendy's, 21, 49, 129
Westmoreland, Nancy, 132
Westmoreland, Preston, 132–133
Westphal, Cindy, 134
Westphal, Michael, 134
Westphal, Paul, 134–135
Westphal, Tori, 134
Whataburger, 135, 137
When in Naples. *See* Maria's When
    in Naples
White, George, 94
White, Jane See, 1
White, Vanna, 89
White Castle, 79
White House, 53, 77

Whitney Foundation, 114
"Wichita Lineman," 14
The Wigwam, 65
Williams, Viola, 120
Williamson, Dorothy McGuire,
    88–89
Williamson, Lowell, 88
Wilson, Robin, 128
Windows on the Green, 19, 115
Woods, Austin, 136
Woods, Cole, 136
Woods, Dylan, 136
Woods, Grant, 1, 136–137
Woods, Lauren, 136
Wright, Frank Lloyd, 92
Wrigley Mansion, 53, 64, 65
Wrigley Mansion's Butternut Squash
    Soup, 65
Writers
    Bombeck, Erma, 10–11
    Cussler, Clive, 1, 30–31
    Davenport, Rita, 36–37
    Guerrero, Zarco, 56–57
    Mackay, Harvey, 78–79
    Steiger, Sam, 122–123
    Trimble, Marshall, 126–127

Xerox, 36

Yarnell, Lorene, 118
Young, Henry VI (Sadim), 38
*Yours Truly, Hugh Downs,* 38

Z Téjas, 71, 73, 87
Zappa, Frank, 64
Zarco's Nana's Albondigas, 57
Zia's, 49
Zucchini, 9, 39
Zum Zum Zum, 57

**EILEEN BAILEY** is a feature columnist for *The Arizona Republic* and former long-time contributor to *Phoenix Magazine.* At her "day job," she is director of marketing/public relations for Phoenix College.

In the 1980s, she founded and published *V Magazine,* a Phoenix/Scottsdale lifestyle monthly, which won Western Publications Association "Maggie" Awards for design and editing. A community activist, Bailey founded the Phoenix College Neighborhood Association, and Kids Read, a program to buy books for at-risk schoolchildren. She is a recent graduate of the Phoenix College Gerontology Program, and is active in Charter 100 and the Osborn Schools Educational Foundation.

A native of Texas, Eileen has lived in Arizona for many years. Besides writing and reading, her interests include her family, cooking, movies, interior design, art collecting, and dancing to live R&B. She lives in a rambling ranch-style home in central Phoenix, where she entertains frequently, "not exquisitely, but often." Her specialty is Eileen's Texas Chainsaw Armadillo Chili.

**DANA LEONARD** graduated from ASU in 1988 with a degree in journalism and spent the next two years as a staff photographer for the *Arizona Business Gazette.* She then worked for *The Phoenix Gazette* for three years, and now works freelance for a variety of editorial and commercial clients.

Dana split her childhood between Tucson, where she was born, and Durango, Colorado. She resides in Phoenix.